GREAT LIVES OBSERVED

Gerald Emanuel Stearn, *General Editor*

EACH VOLUME IN THE SERIES VIEWS THE CHARACTER AND ACHIEVE-
MENT OF A GREAT WORLD FIGURE IN THREE PERSPECTIVES—
THROUGH HIS OWN WORDS, THROUGH THE OPINIONS OF HIS CON-
TEMPORARIES, AND THROUGH RETROSPECTIVE JUDGMENTS—THUS
COMBINING THE INTIMACY OF AUTOBIOGRAPHY, THE IMMEDIACY
OF EYEWITNESS OBSERVATION, AND THE OBJECTIVITY OF MODERN
SCHOLARSHIP.

GEORGE M. FREDRICKSON, *editor of this book, is Associate Professor of History at Northwestern University. Author of* The
Inner Civil War: Northern Intellectuals and the Crisis of the
Union, *he is recipient of a Guggenheim Fellowship (1968–69)
to study American thought on the race question in the nineteenth century.*

Forthcoming volumes in the Great Lives Observed series

Garibaldi, edited by Denis Mack Smith

John F. Kennedy, edited by Barton J. Bernstein

Huey Long, edited by Hugh Davis Graham

Mao, edited by Jerome Ch'en

Joseph McCarthy, edited by Allen Matusow

Booker T. Washington, edited by Emma Lou Thornbrough

Woodrow Wilson, edited by John Braeman

GREAT LIVES OBSERVED

WILLIAM LLOYD
GARRISON

Edited by
GEORGE M. FREDRICKSON

A SPECTRUM BOOK

PRENTICE-HALL, INC., ENGLEWOOD CLIFFS, N.J.

Prentice-Hall International, Inc. (*London*)

Contents

PART ONE
GARRISON LOOKS AT THE WORLD

1

2

3

4

5

6

7

v

PART TWO
GARRISON VIEWED BY HIS CONTEMPORARIES

13

John Greenleaf Whittier (1832): "To William Lloyd Garrison," *73*   Lewis Tappan Praises Garrison (1833), *74* Henry B. Stanton, James G. Birney, and Gamaliel Bailey on Garrison's Controversy with the Clergy (1837), *76* Stanton, Whittier, and Lewis Tappan on the Schisms of 1839–40, *80*

14

Theodore S. Wright: A Tribute to Garrison from a Negro Minister, *85*   Charles B. Ray: Negro Abolitionists and the Schism of 1840, *86*   Frederick Douglass on Garrison, *89* vii

GREAT LIVES OBSERVED

WILLIAM LLOYD GARRISON

Introduction

William Lloyd Garrison did not, in any real sense, lead the American antislavery movement. Abolitionism was a decentralized enterprise subject to local variation and internal factionalism, and Garrison's control of tactics and strategy never extended far beyond the borders of New England (it often was challenged even there). Furthermore, the influence of his brand of abolitionism upon Northern opinion, which never was very great, did not increase with time. His refusal to endorse political activity left him outside the mainstream antislavery efforts of the 1840's and 1850's that resulted in the Free Soil movement and influenced the founding of the Republican Party. But despite these facts and their use by historians in an attempt to discredit the "myth" of Garrison's influence, he remains, and deservedly so, the central figure in the crusade against slavery.

Part of the mystery about Garrison's significance may be resolved by reviewing the facts surrounding his emergence from obscurity. Born in Newburyport, Massachusetts, in 1805, Garrison grew up fatherless and poor. His father, a sailing master with a penchant for strong drink, abandoned the family in 1808. Raised by his mother and by foster parents, he received little formal schooling and eventually was apprenticed to a printer. Educating himself as he set type, Garrison soon became a part-time journalist and then, in 1825, the editor of a weekly newspaper. Unsuccessful in this role, he next moved into the new field of reform journalism, which was developing in the late 1820's as a result of the rise of a variety of benevolent societies and of crusades for human betterment.

In 1828, while editing the *National Philanthropist,* a Boston temperance organ, he met Benjamin Lundy, a Quaker opponent of slavery. Garrison then decided that the cause of the slave was a better center for his reform interests than Demon Rum and agreed to go to Baltimore to become acting editor of Lundy's paper, *The Genius of Universal Emancipation.* Lundy was a supporter of the movement to bring about gradual emancipation through colonizing freed Negroes abroad, but Garrison, although initially accepting this

1

program, soon concluded that the only suitable antislavery platform was immediate emancipation without colonization. In taking this position, he was influenced by the situation in Britain, where the movement for emancipation in the West Indies was triumphing under the slogan "immediate emancipation." As editor of *The Genius,* Garrison took a hard line against slavery and its supporters and eventually was jailed for allegedly libeling a ship owner engaged in the coastal slave trade. The libel judgment brought an end to the joint venture with Lundy, and after forty-nine days in confinement, Garrison returned to Boston, where he began publishing his own antislavery journal, the *Liberator,* in January, 1831.

The *Liberator* was a new departure in the antislavery movement. There had been opposition to slavery previously—much of it a carry-over from the Revolutionary era, when slavery had come under attack as incompatible with the ideals of the Declaration of Independence. But this earlier opposition had been linked, in most cases, with the belief that the two races could not live together in freedom and that emancipation therefore must be gradual and accompanied by the removal of free Negroes from the country. In the *Liberator,* in his speeches, and in his book *Thoughts on African Colonization* (1832), Garrison berated the colonizationists as being, at best, men of little faith and, at worst, covert supporters of slavery. He was not the first antislavery spokesman to attack colonization, but he was the first to make an impression. He wrote in the introductory issue of the *Liberator,* "I will be heard." And heard he was, largely as the result of a harsh and uncompromising mode of expression that publicized his cause through its shock effect and its power to arouse violent opposition. In this way—and perhaps this was the only possible way—he raised the slavery issue in a new form and forced philanthropists and reformers to re-examine their premises. Can we live another moment, he asked, with such a crime as slavery? Does not colonization mean in effect the indefinite prolongation of this curse? Can we be true to the ideals of the Declaration of Independence and also say that the Negro can never be made the equal of the white man as long as he remains within the United States? By asking questions of this sort with a new urgency, Garrison exposed the moral core of the problem as no one else had done. And he succeeded in altering the course of the antislavery movement by reducing colonization to irrelevance.

This work accomplished, he continued to emphasize the moral

dimension, while other men, stimulated by Garrison's initiative to act against slavery, discussed the tactical problems of the movement. The American Anti-Slavery Society, which Garrison helped found in 1833, split in 1840, largely because Garrison insisted on combining feminism and radical pacifism with the crusade against slavery and because other abolitionists were now turning to the kind of overt political activity that he opposed on principle. This schism severely limited Garrison's influence on organized antislavery, but he kept up his agitation. In the 1840's and 1850's, he attacked the Constitution and called for Northern secession from the Union, a position that put him on the extreme left of the antislavery movement but served the function of dramatizing the moral urgency of the cause. Garrison's persistent refusal to come down to the level of practical problems and political exigencies, as well as his tendency to extend the logic of reform into other areas, caused most other abolitionists to part company with him at one time or another. But his primacy as instigator of the movement was unchallenged, and he continued up to the time of emancipation to play an indispensable role as a moral gadfly, keeping the ideal ever in sight of those engaged in confronting the actual.

Besides being the prime mover in freeing abolitionism from the fetter of the colonization scheme and raising it to the level of a color-blind Declaration of Independence, Garrison is important because of the intense opposition he aroused. The South, which was already firmly committed to the defense of slavery before Garrison appeared on the scene, saw him as a real threat, on the erroneous assumption that he had a substantial and growing body of Northern opinion behind him. Impelled by a combination of fear and guilt, Southern extremists strengthened the supports of slavery, launched a militant defense of the institution as "a positive good," and began to argue for its territorial extension. This in turn led Northerners who were offended by the extremism of Garrison to view the South as an aggressive enemy of American (that is, Northern) institutions. The opposition he aroused in the North led to another form of indirect influence; mob action against Garrison and his supporters, like that which took place in Boston in 1835, led prominent Northern moderates to see a danger to civil liberties in efforts to suppress the abolitionists, and their concern for minority rights brought them into alliance, for some purposes, with antislavery zealots whom they otherwise would have spurned. Although Garrison did not guide and control Northern opinion, his initial uncompromising stand helped set off the emotional chain reaction that led to the Civil War and the destruction of slavery.

Since Garrison was the embodiment of the original abolitionist impulse, the question of his motivation and source of inspiration becomes an inescapable problem for anyone desiring to understand the coming of the Civil War. Efforts have been made to describe the abolitionists as disturbed personalities and to characterize the whole antislavery movement in terms of psychological abnormalities. Without doubt, Garrison was self-righteous, dogmatic, lacking in a sense of humor, and prone to think of himself as a martyr to truth in an unbelieving world. In many situations such traits would raise serious questions about a person's mental balance. Yet in Garrison's case, one could argue, they were not fundamentally out of tune with reality, for slavery was an evil to which moral outrage and dogmatic judgment were not inappropriate responses. In addition, those aspects of the Garrisonian posture and style that are hardest for the modern mind to accept were natural results of his education and background. In other words, Garrison successfully internalized a role that his heritage and upbringing clearly favored. Intellectual criticisms may be directed at his mode of thought and action by those whose values differ from his, but the world view it reflected may not be described as a product of personal maladjustment.

The key factor in Garrison's background was the piety and millenarianism spawned in New England by the Great Awakening of the eighteenth century. In the 1740's and 1750's, the American colonies had seen a religious upheaval that gave rise to hopes for an American millennium; zealots of the Awakening had envisioned the transformation of the world through mass conversions and through the organization of an army of believers to crush out the forces of sin and false religion. There resulted a mentality that could easily veer from universal benevolence to uncompromising hatred for the sinner and the hypocrite. This spirit did not die quickly, but continued cropping up in various ways, providing fuel for further awakenings well into the nineteenth century. The radical and individualistic side of the Awakening was preserved most fully in the New England Baptists, many of whom originally had separated from Congregational churches they considered impure or under the guidance of unconverted ministers. Garrison's mother Fanny had been a Baptist convert, a decision that took all the courage of the "come-outer" who is willing to break traditional ties, for it resulted in her being turned out of the house forever by her Episcopalian father. She then had raised her son in the demanding faith and thirst for personal purity that her religious experiences had inculcated. As a young apprentice, Garrison was distinguished from his fellows by a piety that at one point led him to think seriously of becoming a missionary. The essence of his inherited faith was a refusal to compromise with sin, as well as a belief that the millennium would come through the spread of a pure and literal Christianity. Such a gospel was at the heart of Garrison's abolitionist doctrines. From this orientation came his doctrine of "nonresistance," his denial of the authority of all earthly governments, and his rejection of a Constitution that countenanced slavery as "a covenant with Death and an agreement with Hell." The kind of behavior on the part of Garrison and his followers that more moderate abolitionists found most objectionable was strikingly like the behavior of the extremists of the Great Awakening. When the Garrisonians disrupted religious services and called for parishioners to "come out" of proslavery churches, they were following the precedent of the "come-outers" of the previous century. When they attacked the clergy and moderate antislavery men as having impure hearts, they echoed the evangelical attacks upon the "unconverted ministry."

All this, of course, was not simply atavism. It was in tune with important contemporary currents of thought. Given his predispositions, Garrison responded in turn to evangelical crusades like the temperance and peace movements, to an antislavery enterprise that even in its colonization phase had a religious character, and finally, in the late 1830's, to the radical Perfectionism of John Humphrey Noyes, the Christian utopian who believed that the Second Coming already had taken place and that the man of faith could be free from sin and the Law. It seems clear that Garrison can best be understood in religious terms, as a militant Christian anarchist and a legitimate offspring of the left wing of American Protestantism.

Yet Garrison's faith, as extended to include literal acceptance of the Sermon on the Mount and the doctrine of nonresistance to evil, was subject to a severe testing when it came to the question of slave rebellion. It may well be that the aspect of Garrison's thought that is most significant and relevant in our present circumstances is his confronting as a pacifist the reality or possibility of Negro violence. During most of his career, Garrison opposed on principle all use of force. At times, he counseled Southern slaves to be patient and to await the triumph of moral influences. Nevertheless, he could speak approvingly of actual slave revolts, and in 1859 he endorsed John Brown's raid in a manner that set the stage for his support of the Civil War as an antislavery enterprise. There is a certain irreducible inconsistency in his discussions of insurrection and the use of force against slavery, but not as much as is generally supposed. A close reading of Garrison's discussion of insurrection reveals an interesting, if not wholly satisfactory, effort to resolve the dilemma of the pacifist who sympathizes with the victims of oppression.

Garrison recognized, first of all, that slavery itself was a form of violence directed against the Negro. He hoped, undoubtedly, to end slavery by moral suasion but, with all his belief in human perfectibility, was not absolutely certain that this would happen. Another part of his religious heritage recognized divine judgments upon sinful nations, and he never ruled out the possibility that slavery would go down in blood as a judgment upon those who had refused to heed a moral appeal. (It was in precisely these terms that he was to support the Northern effort in the Civil War.) Certain that the violence of the oppressor led inevitably to the violence of the oppressed, Garrison felt justified in calling attention, as part of his effort to convince slaveholders of the need for immediate steps toward emancipation, to the danger of slave insurrection. In believing that such an appeal would be effective, he grossly underestimated the tenacity of the Southern commitment to slavery; if anything, his appeals contributed to increased coercion in the South. His belief that oppression leads inevitably to resistance might also be questioned on the ground that oppression can be so severe that there is little or no chance for rebellion, as seems, by and large, to have been the case with Southern slavery. But Garrison lived in a revolutionary world not totally unlike our own, and he could not escape thinking in terms of revolutionary precedents. The French and the American revolutions at the end of the previous century had been followed by the European uprisings of 1830, and Garrison was clearly in sympathy with the results of these movements if not with their methods. He pointed out in a speech to a free Negro audience in 1831:

The signs of the times do indeed show forth great and glorious and sudden in changes in the condition of the oppressed. The whole firmament is tremulous with an excess of light; the earth is moved out of its place; the wave of revolution is dashing to pieces ancient and mighty empires; the hearts of tyrants are beginning to fail them for fear; and for looking forward to those things which are to come upon earth.

Believing, as he did, that the millennium would come only with the abjuration of the use of force in all its forms, he wished to take a personal stand based upon the pure ideals of the Coming Kingdom, but he made clear where his sympathies would be in the case of an actual slave rebellion. As he pointed out in his speech on John Brown, "Wherever there is a contest between the oppressed and the oppressor,—the weapons being equal between the parties,—God knows my heart must be with the oppressed, and always against the oppressor." He went on, in that speech, to argue that the use of force by those striving for elemental freedom was actually a step in the direction of "the sublime platform of non-resistance," because it was "God's way of dealing retribution on the head of the tyrant" and would presumably lead to conditions that would make the use of force unnecessary. "Rather than see men wear their chains in a cowardly and servile spirit," he concluded, "I would, as an advocate of peace, much rather see them breaking the head of the tyrant with their chains. Give me, as a non-resistant, Bunker Hill, and Lexington, and Concord, rather than the cowardice and servility of a slave plantation." With statements like these Garrison continually challenged the consistency of the American majority, which reverenced the American Revolution and was sympathetic to the recent European uprisings but regarded a slave rebellion as a monstrous crime. He maintained over and over again that only a man like himself who had rejected the authority of a government that condoned slavery, and was thereby disassociated from the machinery of oppression, had a moral right to condemn slave resistance. Indeed only a people that collectively had ceased to practice violence against the Negro in the form of slavery had a right to expect anything but violence from the Negro.

Although Garrison condoned or even welcomed slave uprisings as better than subservience to tyranny, he clearly and unequivocally ruled out the use of force, public or private, to right the inequities of a society like that of the North, which was based on "free institutions." He recognized that Northern free Negroes suffered from discrimination and segregation, but to them he counseled only "Christian resignation" and "self-help" in an effort to win the approval and respect of their white neighbors. When confronting English Chartists and other labor radicals, he made clear his belief that the grievances of the working men did not constitute "industrial slavery" and were no cause for new forms of collective action. In the first issue of the *Liberator*, he denied the existence of conflict between wealth and poverty, or between labor and capital, and demonstrated his faith in an industrial order held together by the benevolence of the rich and the cultivation of Protestant virtues by the poor. Hence, Garrison's oblique support of revolution was limited to revolution against flagrant political despotism, whether of a European king or of a Southern plantation owner. He foresaw no possible need for revolutionary action in a formally democratic and egalitarian society in which, despite occasional harassment of those with unpopular opinions, there were freedom of expression and the possibility of influencing men's minds through peaceful agitation.

Garrison's implicit theory of progress was, therefore, a three-stage affair. From despotism, a people moved up to a republican *laissez-faire* society, generally but regrettably through the use of force; from this formally democratic society, a genuinely free society without government or coercion emerged, brought about by the peaceful agitation and moral suasion that was now possible. What Garrison could not foresee before 1861, and failed to recognize thereafter, was that history was not moving in the millennial direction he had charted for it, and that subtler forms of oppression would develop in the bosom of a slaveless republic that would raise new doubts as to whether entrenched injustice could be eliminated by appeals to conscience and morality.

Chronology of the Life of Garrison

1805	(December 10) Born in Newburyport, Massachusetts, the son of Abijah and Fanny Garrison.
1808	Desertion of the family by Abijah Garrison.
1814—18	Apprenticed in turn to a shoemaker, a cabinetmaker, and a printer.
1818—25	Serves as an apprentice-printer with the Newburyport *Herald*.
1826	Becomes editor of the Essex (County) *Free Press*.
1828—29	Serves successively as the editor of the *National Philanthropist* (Boston) and the *Journal of the Times* (Bennington, Vt.).
1829—30	Co-editor of the *Genius of Universal Emancipation* (Baltimore).
1830	Is jailed for libel in Baltimore.
1831	(January 1) Begins publication of the *Liberator*. (August) Nat Turner's insurrection.
1832	Founding of the New England Anti-Slavery Society. Publication of *Thoughts on African Colonization*.
1833	First trip to England. Founding of the American Anti-Slavery Society.
1835	(October 21) Mobbed in Boston.
1835—37	Controversy with the New England clergy.
1837—38	Espouses "non-resistance" and women's rights.
1840	Captures control of the American Anti-Slavery Society. Attends International Anti-Slavery Convention in London but refuses to take a seat because of discrimination against women.
1844	American Anti-Slavery Society takes a stand in favor of disunion.
1846—47	The Mexican War.
1847	First speaking tour of Ohio.
1850	Opposes the Compromise of 1850 and the Fugitive Slave Law. Attacked by "the Rynders mob" in New York City.
1854—56	The Kansas-Nebraska Act and Bleeding Kansas.
1859	Defense of John Brown's raid.
1860—61	Election of Lincoln, secession of the South, beginning of the Civil War.

1861–62	Endorses the war but is critical of Lincoln until after the preliminary Emancipation Proclamation (September, 1862).
1862–63	Hails the Emancipation Proclamation, supports Lincoln, sees his own work as over.
1864	Breaks with Wendell Phillips and the radicals in the American Anti-Slavery Society.
1865	(December 29) The *Liberator* ceases publication.
1866–67	Denounces President Johnson and upholds the Radicals on Reconstruction.
1879	(May 24) Dies in New York City.

PART ONE

GARRISON LOOKS AT THE WORLD

1

Fourth of July Address, 1829[1]

This was Garrison's first major public address and the first full statement of his antislavery commitment. But its approach to abolition was moderate in comparison with the position he took soon afterwards. At this time, Garrison still was favorably disposed toward the colonization movement, and the address, given at Park Street Church in Boston, was expressly for the benefit of the American Colonization Society. What follows is a substantial excerpt from a speech that took over an hour.

I speak not as a partisan or an opponent of any man or measure, when I say that our politics are rotten to the core. *We* boast of our freedom, who go shackled to the polls, year after year, by tens, and hundreds, and thousands! *We* talk of free agency, who are the veriest machines—the merest automata—in the hands of unprincipled jugglers! *We* prate of integrity, and virtue, and independence, who sell our birthright for office, and who, nine times in ten, do not get Esau's bargain—no, not even a mess of pottage! Is it republicanism to say, that the majority can do no wrong? Then I am not a republican. Is it aristocracy to say, that the people sometimes shamefully abuse their high trust? Then I am an aristocrat. It is not the appreciation, but the abuse of liberty, to withdraw altogether from the polls, or to visit them merely as a matter of form, without carefully

[1] From Wendell Phillips Garrison and Francis Jackson Garrison, *William Lloyd Garrison: The Story of His Life* (New York, 1885), I, 127–37. (Footnotes by Garrison and Garrison.)

investigating the merits of candidates. The republican does not bear a charmed life: our prescriptions administered through the medium of the ballot-box—the mouth of the political body—may kill or cure, according to the nature of the disease and our wisdom in applying the remedy. It is possible that a people may bear the title of freemen who execute the work of slaves. To the dullest observers of the signs of the times, it must be apparent that we are rapidly approximating to this condition. . . .

But there is another evil, which, if we had to contend against nothing else, should make us quake for the issue. It is a gangrene preying upon our vitals—an earthquake rumbling under our feet—a mine accumulating materials for a national catastrophe. It should make this a day of fasting and prayer, not of boisterous merriment and idle pageantry—a day of great lamentation, not of congratulatory joy. It should spike every cannon, and haul down every banner. Our garb should be sackcloth—our heads bowed in the dust—our supplications, for the pardon and assistance of Heaven.

Last week this city was made breathless by a trial of considerable magnitude. The court chamber was inundated for hours, day after day, with a dense and living tide which swept along like the rush of a mountain torrent. Tiers of human bodies were piled up to the walls, with almost miraculous condensation and ingenuity. It seemed as if men abhorred a vacuum equally with Nature: they would suspend themselves, as it were, by a nail, and stand upon air with the aid of a peg. Although it was a barren, ineloquent subject, and the crowd immense, there was no perceptible want of interest—no evidence of impatience. The cause was important, involving the reputation of a distinguished citizen. There was a struggle for mastery between two giants—a test of strength in tossing mountains of law. The excitement was natural.[2]

I stand up here in a more solemn court, to assist in a far greater cause; not to impeach the character of one man, but of a whole people; not to recover the sum of a hundred thousand dollars, but to obtain the liberation of two millions of wretched, degraded beings, who are pining in hopeless bondage—over whose sufferings scarcely an eye weeps, or a heart melts, or a tongue pleads either to God or man. I

---

[2] The case was that of Farnum, Executor of Tuttle Hubbard, *vs.* Brooks, and was heard in the Mass. Supreme Court. The "two giants" in opposition were William Wirt, ex-Attorney-General of the United States, and Daniel Webster. Wirt's eloquence made a great impression. (Boston *Traveller,* June 23, 30, 1829; *Columbian Centinel,* June 27.)

regret that a better advocate had not been found, to enchain your attention and to warm your blood. Whatever fallacy, however, may appear in the argument, there is no flaw in the indictment; what the speaker lacks, the cause will supply.

Sirs, I am not come to tell you that slavery is a curse, debasing in its effect, cruel in its operation, fatal in its continuance. The day and the occasion require no such revelation. I do not claim the discovery as my own, that "all men are born equal," and that among their inalienable rights are "life, liberty, and the pursuit of happiness." Were I addressing any other than a free and Christian assembly, the enforcement of this truth might be pertinent. Neither do I intend to analyze the horrors of slavery for your inspection, nor to freeze your blood with authentic recitals of savage cruelty. Nor will time allow me to explore even a furlong of that immense wilderness of suffering which remains unsubdued in our land. I take it for granted that the existence of these evils is acknowledged, if not rightly understood. My object is to define and enforce our duty, as Christians and Philanthropists.

On a subject so exhaustless, it will be impossible, in the moiety of an address, to unfold all the facts which are necessary to its full development. In view of it, my heart swells up like a living fountain, which time cannot exhaust, for it is perpetual. Let this be considered as a preface of a noble work, which your inventive sympathies must elaborate and complete.

I assume as distinct and defensible propositions,

I. That the slaves of this country, whether we consider their moral, intellectual or social condition, are preëminently entitled to the prayers, and sympathies, and charities, of the American people; and their claims for redress are as strong as those of any Americans could be in a similar condition.

II. That, as the free States—by which I mean non-slaveholding States—are constitutionally involved in the guilt of slavery, by adhering to a national compact that sanctions it; and in the danger, by liability to be called upon for aid in case of insurrection; they have the right to remonstrate against its continuance, and it is their duty to assist in its overthrow.

III. That no justificative plea for the perpetuity of slavery can be found in the condition of its victims; and no barrier against our righteous interference, in the laws which authorize the buying, selling and possessing of slaves, nor in the hazard of a collision with slaveholders.

IV. That education and freedom will elevate our colored population to a rank with the white—making them useful, intelligent and
peaceable citizens.

In the first place, it will be readily admitted, that it is the duty of
every nation primarily to administer relief to its own necessities, to
cure its own maladies, to instruct its own children, and to watch over
its own interests. He is "worse than an infidel" who neglects his own
household, and squanders his earnings upon strangers; and the policy
of that nation is unwise which seeks to proselyte other portions of the
globe at the expense of its safety and happiness. Let me not be misunderstood. My benevolence is neither contracted nor selfish. I pity
that man whose heart is not larger than a whole continent. I despise
the littleness of that patriotism which blusters only for its own rights,
and, stretched to its utmost dimensions, scarcely covers its native
territory; which adopts as its creed the right to act independently,
even to the verge of licentiousness, without restraint, and to tyrannize
wherever it can with impunity. This sort of patriotism is common. I
suspect the reality, and deny the productiveness, of that piety which
confines its operations to a particular spot—if that spot be less than
the whole earth; nor scoops out, in every direction, new channels for
the waters of life. Christian charity, while it "begins at home," goes
abroad in search of misery. It is as copious as the sun in heaven. It
does not, like the Nile, make a partial inundation, and then withdraw;
but it perpetually overflows, and fertilizes every barren spot. It is restricted only by the exact number of God's suffering creatures. But I
mean to say, that, while we are aiding and instructing foreigners, we
ought not to forget our own degraded countrymen; that neither duty
nor honesty requires us to defraud ourselves that we may enrich others.

The condition of the slaves, in a religious point of view, is deplor-
able, entitling them to a higher consideration, on our part, than any
other race; higher than the Turks or Chinese, for they have the privileges of instruction; higher than the Pagans, for they are not dwellers
in a gospel land; higher than our red men of the forest, for we do not
bind them with gyves, nor treat them as chattels.

And here let me ask, What has Christianity done, by direct effort,
for our slave population? Comparatively nothing. She has explored
the isles of the ocean for objects of commiseration; but, amazing stu-
pidity! she can gaze without emotion on a multitude of miserable
beings at home, large enough to constitute a nation of freemen, whom
tyranny has heathenized by law. In her public services they are seldom

remembered, and in her private donations they are forgotten. From one end of the country to the other, her charitable societies form golden links of benevolence, and scatter their contributions like raindrops over a parched heath; but they bring no sustenance to the perishing slave. The blood of souls is upon her garments, yet she heeds not the stain. The clankings of the prisoner's chains strike upon her ear, but they cannot penetrate her heart.

I have said that the claims of the slaves for redress are as strong as those of any Americans could be, in a similar condition. Does any man deny the position? The proof, then, is found in the fact, that a very large proportion of our colored population were born on our soil, and are therefore entitled to all the privileges of American citizens. This is their country by birth, not by adoption. Their children possess the same inherent and unalienable rights as ours, and it is a crime of the blackest dye to load them with fetters.

Every Fourth of July, our Declaration of Independence is produced, with a sublime indignation, to set forth the tyranny of the mother country, and to challenge the admiration of the world. But what a pitiful detail of grievances does this document present, in comparison with the wrongs which our slaves endure! In the one case, it is hardly the plucking of a hair from the head; in the other, it is the crushing of a live body on the wheel—the stings of the wasp contrasted with the tortures of the Inquisition. Before God, I must say, that such a glaring contradiction as exists between our creed and practice the annals of six thousand years cannot parallel. In view of it, I am ashamed of my country. I am sick of our unmeaning declamation in praise of liberty and equality; of our hypocritical cant about the unalienable rights of man. I could not, for my right hand, stand up before a European assembly, and exult that I am an American citizen, and denounce the usurpations of a kingly government as wicked and unjust; or, should I make the attempt, the recollection of my country's barbarity and despotism would blister my lips, and cover my cheeks with burning blushes of shame.

Will this be termed a rhetorical flourish? Will any man coldly accuse me of intemperate zeal? I will borrow, then, a ray of humanity from one of the brightest stars in our American galaxy, whose light will gather new effulgence to the end of time. "This, sirs, is a cause that would be dishonored and betrayed if I contented myself with appealing only to the understanding. It is too cold, and its processes are too slow for the occasion. I desire to thank God that, since he has given me an intellect so fallible, he has impressed upon me an instinct that is sure. On a question of shame and honor—liberty and oppression—reasoning is sometimes useless, and worse. I feel the decision in my pulse: if it throws no light upon the brain, it kindles a fire at the heart.". . .

I come to my second proposition:—the right of the free States to remonstrate against the continuance, and to assist in the overthrow of slavery.

This, I am aware, is a delicate subject, surrounded with many formidable difficulties. But if delay only adds to its intricacy, wherefore shun an immediate investigation? I know that we, of the North, affectedly believe that we have no local interest in the removal of this great evil; that the slave States can take care of themselves, and that any proffered assistance, on our part, would be rejected as impertinent, dictatorial or meddlesome; and that we have no right to lift up even a note of remonstrance. But I believe that these opinions are crude, preposterous, dishonorable, unjust. Sirs, this is a business in which, as members of one great family, we have a common interest; but we take no responsibility, either individually or collectively. Our hearts are cold—our blood stagnates in our veins. We act, in relation to the slaves, as if they were something lower than the brutes that perish.

On this question, I ask no support from the injunction of Holy Writ, which says:—"therefore all things whatsoever ye would that men should do to you, do ye even so to them: for this is the law and the prophets." I throw aside the common dictates of humanity. I assert the right of the free States to demand a gradual abolition of slavery, because, by its continuance, they participate in the guilt thereof, and are threatened with ultimate destruction; because they are bound to watch over the interests of the whole country, without reference to territorial divisions; because their white population is nearly double that of the slave States, and the voice of this overwhelming majority should be potential; because they are now deprived of their just influence in the councils of the nation; because it is absurd and anti-republican to suffer property to be represented as men, and *vice versa*.[3] Because it gives the South an unjust ascendancy over other portions of territory, and a power which may be perverted on every occasion. . . .

Now I say that, on the broad system of equal rights, this monstrous

[3] By the three-fifths representation clause of the Federal Constitution, Art. I., Sec. ii., 3.

inequality should no longer be tolerated. If it cannot be speedily put down—not by force, but by fair persuasion; if we are always to remain shackled by unjust Constitutional provisions, when the emergency that imposed them has long since passed away; if we must share in the guilt and danger of destroying the bodies and souls of men, *as the price of our Union;* if the slave States will haughtily spurn our assistance, and refuse to consult the general welfare; then the fault is not ours if a separation eventually take place. . . .

It may be objected, that the laws of the slave States form insurmountable barriers to any interference on our part.

Answer. I grant that we have not the right, and I trust not the disposition, to use coercive measures. But do these laws hinder our prayers, or obstruct the flow of our sympathies? Cannot our charities alleviate the condition of the slave, and perhaps break his fetters? Can we not operate upon public sentiment, (the lever that can move the moral world,) by way of remonstrance, advice, or entreaty? Is Christianity so powerful that she can tame the red men of our forests, and abolish the Burman caste, and overthrow the gods of Paganism, and liberate lands over which the darkness of Superstition has lain for ages; and yet so weak, in her own dwelling-place, that she can make no impression upon her civil code? Can she contend successfully with cannibals, and yet be conquered by her own children?

Suppose that, by a miracle, the slaves should suddenly become white. Would you shut your eyes upon their sufferings, and calmly talk of Constitutional limitations? No; your voice would peal in the ears of the taskmasters like deep thunder; you would carry the Constitution by force, if it could not be taken by treaty; patriotic assemblies would congregate at the corners of every street; the old Cradle of Liberty would rock to a deeper tone than ever echoed therein at British aggression; the pulpit would acquire new and unusual eloquence from our holy religion. The argument, that these white slaves are degraded, would not then obtain. You would say, it is enough that they are white, and in bondage, and they ought immediately to be set free. You would multiply your schools of instruction, and your temples of worship, and rely on them for security. . . .

But the plea is prevalent, that any interference by the free States, however benevolent or cautious it might be, would only irritate and inflame the jealousies of the South, and retard the cause of emancipation. If any man believes that slavery can be abolished without a struggle with the worst passions of human nature, quietly, harmoniously, he cherishes a delusion. It can never be done, unless the age of miracles return. No; we must expect a collision, full of sharp asperities and bitterness. We shall have to contend with the insolence, and pride, and selfishness, of many a heartless being. But these can be easily conquered by meekness, and perseverance, and prayer.

Sirs, the prejudices of the North are stronger than those of the South;—they bristle, like so many bayonets, around the slaves;—they forge and rivet the chains of the nation. Conquer them, and the victory is won. The enemies of emancipation take courage from our criminal timidity. They have justly stigmatized us, even on the floor of Congress, with the most contemptuous epithets. We are (they say) their "white slaves," [4] afraid of our own shadows, who have been driven back to the wall again and again; who stand trembling under their whips; who turn pale, retreat, and surrender, at a talismanic threat to dissolve the Union. . . .

It is often despondingly said, that the evil of slavery is beyond our control. Dreadful conclusion, that puts the seal of death upon our country's existence! If we cannot conquer the monster in his infancy, while his cartilages are tender and his limbs powerless, how shall we escape his wrath when he goes forth a gigantic cannibal, seeking whom he may devour? If we cannot safely unloose two millions of slaves now, how shall we bind upwards of TWENTY MILLIONS at the close of the present century? But there is no cause for despair. We have seen how readily, and with what ease, that horrid gorgon, Intemperance, has been checked in his ravages. Let us take courage. Moral influence, when in vigorous exercise, is irresistible. It has an immortal essence. It can no more be trod out of existence by the iron foot of time, or by the ponderous march of iniquity, than matter can be annihilated. It may disappear for a time; but it lives in some shape or other, in some place or other, and will rise with renovated strength. Let us, then, be up and doing. In the simple and stirring language of the stout-hearted Lundy, "all the friends of the cause must go to work, keep to work, hold on, and never give up."

If it be still objected, that it would be dangerous to liberate the present race of blacks:

I answer—the emancipation of all the slaves of this generation is

---

[4] In Henry Adams's "Life of John Randolph" we read (p. 281): "On another occasion, he [Randolph] is reported as saying of the people of the North, 'We do not govern them by our black slaves, but by their own white slaves.' "

most assuredly out of the question. The fabric, which now towers above the Alps, must be taken away brick by brick, and foot by foot, till it is reduced so low that it may be overturned without burying the nation in its ruins. Years may elapse before the completion of the achievement; generations of blacks may go down to the grave, manacled and lacerated, without a hope for their children; the philanthropists who are now pleading in behalf of the oppressed, may not live to witness the dawn which will precede the glorious day of universal emancipation; but the work will go on—laborers in the cause will multiply—new resources will be discovered—the victory will be obtained, worth the desperate struggle of a thousand years. Or, if defeat follow, woe to the safety of this people! The nation will be shaken as if by a mighty earthquake. A cry of horror, a cry of revenge, will go up to heaven in the darkness of midnight, and re-echo from every cloud. Blood will flow like water—the blood of guilty men, and of innocent women and children. Then will be heard lamentations and weeping, such as will blot out the remembrance of the horrors of St. Domingo. The terrible judgments of an incensed God will complete the catastrophe of republican America.

And since so much is to be done for our country; since so many prejudices are to be dispelled, obstacles vanquished, interests secured, blessings obtained; since the cause of emancipation must progress heavily, and meet with much unhallowed opposition,—why delay the work? There must be a beginning, and now is a propitious time— perhaps the last opportunity that will be granted us by a long-suffering God. No temporizing, lukewarm measures will avail aught. We must put our shoulders to the wheel, and heave with our united strength. Let us not look coldly on and see our Southern brethren[5] contending single-handed against an all-powerful foe—faint, weary, borne down to the earth. We are all alike guilty. Slavery is strictly a national sin. New-England money has been expended in buying human flesh; New-England ships have been freighted with sable victims; New-England men have assisted in forging the fetters of those who groan in bondage.

I call upon the ambassadors of Christ everywhere to make known this proclamation: "Thus saith the Lord God of the Africans, Let this people go, that they may serve me." I ask them to "proclaim liberty to the captives, and the opening of the prison to them that are bound"—

[5] An allusion to the few anti-slavery societies among the Friends in some of the Southern States.

to light up a flame of philanthropy that shall burn till all Africa be redeemed from the night of moral death, and the song of deliverance be heard throughout her borders.

I call upon the churches of the living God to lead in this great enterprise.[6] If the soul be immortal, priceless, save it from remediless woe. Let them combine their energies, and systematize their plans, for the rescue of suffering humanity. Let them pour out their supplications to heaven in behalf of the slave. Prayer is omnipotent: its breath can melt adamantine rocks—its touch can break the stoutest chains. Let anti-slavery charity-boxes stand uppermost among those for missionary, tract and educational purposes. On this subject, Christians have been asleep; let them shake off their slumbers, and arm for the holy contest.

I call upon our New-England women to form charitable associations to relieve the degraded of their sex. As yet, an appeal to their sympathies was never made in vain. They outstrip us in every benevolent race. Females are doing much for the cause at the South; let their example be imitated, and their exertions surpassed, at the North.

I call upon our citizens to assist in establishing auxiliary colonization societies in every State, county and town. I implore their direct and liberal patronage to the parent society.

I call upon the great body of newspaper editors to keep this subject constantly before their readers; to sound the trumpet of alarm, and to plead eloquently for the rights of man. They must give the tone to public sentiment. One press may ignite twenty; a city may warm a State; a State may impart a generous heat to a whole country.

I call upon the American people to enfranchise a spot over which they hold complete sovereignty; to cleanse that worse than Augean stable, the District of Columbia, from its foul impurities. I ask them to sustain Congress in any future efforts to colonize the colored population of the States. I conjure them to select those as Representatives who are not too ignorant to know, too blind to see, nor too timid to perform their duty.

I will say, finally, that I despair of the republic while slavery exists therein. If I look up to God for success, no smile of mercy or forgive-

___

[6] So Daniel Webster, in his Plymouth oration, Dec. 22, 1820, of the African slave-trade and of New-England complicity with it: "I invoke the ministers of our religion, that they proclaim its denunciation of these crimes, and add its solemn sanctions to the authority of human laws. If the pulpit be silent whenever or wherever there may be a sinner bloody with this guilt within the hearing of its voice, the pulpit is false to its trust" (Works, 1:46).

ness dispels the gloom of futurity; if to our own resources, they are daily diminishing; if to all history, our destruction is not only possible, but almost certain. Why should we slumber at this momentous crisis? If our hearts were dead to every throb of humanity; if it were lawful to oppress, where power is ample; still, if we had any regard for our safety and happiness, we should strive to crush the Vampire which is feeding upon our life-blood. All the selfishness of our nature cries aloud for a better security. Our own vices are too strong for us, and keep us in perpetual alarm; how, in addition to these, shall we be able to contend successfully with millions of armed and desperate men, as we must eventually, if slavery do not cease?

2

Opening Statement of the First Issue of the Liberator[1]

This is the famous salutory address that introduced the first issue of the Liberator *(January 1, 1831). It shocked many by its severity and forthrightness and became the most famous and widely quoted utterance of Garrison's career.*

TO THE PUBLIC

In the month of August, I issued proposals for publishing "THE LIBERATOR" in Washington City; but the enterprise, though hailed in different sections of the country, was palsied by public indifference. Since that time, the removal of the *Genius of Universal Emancipation* to the Seat of Government has rendered less imperious the establishment of a similar periodical in that quarter.

During my recent tour for the purpose of exciting the minds of the people by a series of discourses on the subject of slavery, every place that I visited gave fresh evidence of the fact, that a greater revolution in public sentiment was to be effected in the free States—*and particularly in New-England*—than at the South. I found contempt more bitter, opposition more active, detraction more relentless, prejudice more stubborn, and apathy more frozen, than among slave-owners themselves. Of course, there were individual exceptions to the contrary. This state of things afflicted, but did not dishearten me. I determined, at every hazard, to lift up the standard of emancipation in the eyes of the nation, *within sight of Bunker Hill and in the birthplace of liberty*. That standard is now unfurled; and long may it float, unhurt by the spoliations of time or the missiles of a desperate foe—yea, till every chain be broken, and every bondman set free! Let Southern oppressors tremble—let their secret abettors tremble—let their Northern apologists tremble—let all the enemies of the persecuted blacks tremble.

I deem the publication of my original Prospectus unnecessary, as it

[1] From the *Liberator* (Boston), January 1, 1831.

has obtained a wide circulation. The principles therein inculcated will be steadily pursued in this paper, excepting that I shall not array myself as the political partisan of any man. In defending the great cause of human rights, I wish to derive the assistance of all religions and of all parties.

Assenting to the "self-evident truth" maintained in the American Declaration of Independence, "that all men are created equal, and endowed by their Creator with certain inalienable rights—among which are life, liberty and the pursuit of happiness," I shall strenuously contend for the immediate enfranchisement of our slave population. In Park-Street Church, on the Fourth of July, 1829, in an address on slavery, I unreflectingly assented to the popular but pernicious doctrine of *gradual* abolition. I seize this opportunity to make a full and unequivocal recantation, and thus publicly to ask pardon of my God, of my country, and of my brethren the poor slaves, for having uttered a sentiment so full of timidity, injustice, and absurdity. A similar recantation, from my pen, was published in the *Genius of Universal Emancipation* at Baltimore, in September, 1829. My conscience is now satisfied.

I am aware that many object to the severity of my language; but is there not cause for severity? I *will be* as harsh as truth, and as uncompromising as justice. On this subject, I do not wish to think, or speak, or write, with moderation. No! no! Tell a man whose house is on fire to give a moderate alarm; tell him to moderately rescue his wife from the hands of the ravisher; tell the mother to gradually extricate her babe from the fire into which it has fallen;—but urge me not to use moderation in a cause like the present. I am in earnest—I will not equivocate—I will not excuse—I will not retreat a single inch—AND I WILL BE HEARD. The apathy of the people is enough to make every statue leap from its pedestal, and to hasten the resurrection of the dead.

It is pretended, that I am retarding the cause of emancipation by the coarseness of my invective and the precipitancy of my measures. *The charge is not true.* On this question my influence,—humble as it is,—is felt at this moment to a considerable extent, and shall be felt in coming years—not perniciously, but beneficially—not as a curse, but as a blessing; and posterity will bear testimony that I was right. I desire to thank God, that he enables me to disregard "the fear of man which bringeth a snare," and to speak his truth in its simplicity and power. . . .

3

Editorial on Nat Turner's Insurrection[1]

One of the first indications of Garrison's complex atti-
tude toward slave rebellion was this editorial on the Nat Turner
insurrection from the Liberator *of September 3, 1831. This re-*
volt, which had taken place in Southampton County, Virginia,
late in August, was the most sustained and violent uprising in the
history of American slavery and resulted in the death of fifty-five
whites.

What we have long predicted,—at the peril of being stigmatized
as an alarmist and declaimer,—has commenced its fulfilment. The first
step of the earthquake, which is ultimately to shake down the fabric
of oppression, leaving not one stone upon the other, has been made.
The first drops of blood, which are but the prelude to a deluge from
the gathering clouds, have fallen. The first flash of lightning, which
is to ignite and consume, has been felt. The first wailings of a bereave-
ment, which is to clothe the earth in sackcloth, have broken upon our
ears.

In the first number of the Liberator, we alluded to the hour of
vengeance in the following lines:

> Wo if it come with storm, and blood, and fire,
>> When midnight darkness veils the earth and sky!
> *Wo to the innocent babe*—the guilty sire—
>> *Mother and daughter*—friends of kindred tie!
>> *Stranger and citizen alike shall die!*
> Red-handed Slaughter his revenge shall feed,
>> And Havoc yell his ominious death-cry,
>> And wild Despair in vain for mercy plead—
>> While hell itself shall shrink and sicken at the deed!

[1] From the *Liberator* (Boston), September 3, 1831.

Read the account of the insurrection in Virginia, and say whether our prophecy be not fulfilled. What was poetry—imagination—in January, is now a bloody reality. "Wo to the innocent babe—to mother and daughter!" Is it not true? Turn again to the record of slaughter! Whole families have been cut off—not a mother, not a daughter, not a babe left. Dreadful retaliation! "The dead bodies of white and black lying just as they were slain, unburied"—the oppressor and the oppressed equal at last in death—what a spectacle!

True, the rebellion is quelled. Those of the slaves who were not killed in combat, have been secured, and the prison is crowded with victims destined for the gallows!

> "Yet laugh not in your carnival of crime
> Too proudly, ye oppressors!"

You have seen, it is to be feared, but the beginning of sorrows. All the blood which has been shed will be required at your hands. At your hands alone? No—but at the hands of the people of New-England and of all the free states. The crime of oppression is national. The south is only the agent in this guilty traffic. But, remember! the same causes are at work which must inevitably produce the same effects; and when the contest shall have again begun, it must be again a war of extermination. In the present instance, no quarters have been asked or given.

But we have killed and routed them now—we can do it again and again—we are invincible! A dastardly triumph, well becoming a nation of oppressors. Detestable complacency, that can think, without emotion, of the extermination of the blacks! We have the power to kill *all*—let us, therefore, continue to apply the whip and forget new fetters!

In his fury against the revolters, who will remember their wrongs? What will it avail them, though the catalogue of their sufferings, dripping with warm blood fresh from their lacerated bodies, be held up to extenuate their conduct? It is enough that the victims were black—that circumstance makes them less precious than the dogs which have been slain in our streets! They were black—brutes, pretending to be men—legions of curses on their memories! They were black—God made them to serve us!

Ye patriotic hypocrites! ye panegyrists of Frenchmen, Greeks, and Poles! ye fustian declaimers for liberty! ye valient sticklers for equal

rights among yourselves! ye haters of aristocracy! ye assailants of mon-
archies! ye republican nullifiers! ye treasonable disunionists! be dumb!
Cast no reproach upon the conduct of the slaves, but let your lips and
cheeks wear the blisters of condemnation!

Ye accuse the pacific friends of emancipation of instigating the slaves
to revolt. Take back the charge as a foul slander. The slaves need no
incentives at our hands. They will find them in their stripes—in their
emaciated bodies—in their ceaseless toil—in their ignorant minds—
in every field, in every valley, on every hill-top and mountain, wherever
you and your fathers have fought for liberty—in your speeches, your
conversations, your celebrations, your pamphlets, your newspapers—
voices in the air, sounds from across the ocean, invitations to resistance
above, below, around them! What more do they need? Surrounded by
such influences, and smarting under their newly made wounds, is it
wonderful that they should rise to contend—as other "heroes" have
contended—for their lost rights? It is *not* wonderful.

In all that we have written, is there aught to justify the excesses of
the slaves? No. Nevertheless, they deserve no more censure than the
Greeks in destroying the Turks, or the Poles in exterminating the
Russians, or our fathers in slaughtering the British. Dreadful, indeed,
is the standard erected by worldly patriotism!

For ourselves, we are horror-struck at the late tidings. We have
exerted our utmost efforts to avert the calamity. We have warned our
countrymen of the danger of persisting in their unrighteous conduct.
We have preached to the slaves the pacific precepts of Jesus Christ.
We have appealed to christians, philanthropists and patriots, for their
assistance to accomplish the great work of national redemption through
the agency of moral power—of public opinion—of individual duty.
How have we been received? We have been threatened, proscribed,
vilified and imprisoned—a laughing-stock and a reproach. Do we
falter, in view of these things? Let time answer. If we have been
hitherto urgent, and bold, and denunciatory in our efforts,—hereafter
we shall grow vehement and active with the increase of danger. We
shall cry, in trumpet tones, night and day,—Wo to this guilty land,
unless she speedily repents of her evil doings! The blood of millions
of her sons cries aloud for redress! IMMEDIATE EMANCIPATION
can alone save her from the vengeance of Heaven, and cancel the debt
of ages!

4

First Anniversary Editorial in the Liberator[1]

*This editorial, entitled "The Liberator and Slavery,"
marked the first anniversary of the journal with a powerful statement of Garrison's sympathy with the revolutionary movements
taking place throughout the world. It also raised for the first
time the question of the value of a Union and of a Constitution
that involved the North in "the guilt and danger of slavery."*

The past has been a year more than ordinarily eventful to this
country and the world. Henceforth there is to be no peace on the
earth—no cessation of revolutionary movements—no exhausted im-
becility—until unjust rule be at an end; until personal thraldom be
broken; until thrones be scattered in ashes to the winds; until heridi-
tary titles and distinctions be effaced; until knowledge be diffused as
freely as sun-light, and be as readily inhaled by all classes of the
people as the vital atmosphere; until landed monopolies be distrib-
uted in equitable shares; until all labor be voluntary, receive its just
remuneration, be protected in its own earnings, be a crown of honor
and not a mark of servitude; until every government be elective and
republican; until the right to worship God, according to the dictates
of every man's conscience, be secured; until, in short, freedom of
thought and speech and writing—freedom of choice—freedom of action—be not only the inalienable right but the positive exercise of
every rational creature. The Spirit of Liberty is no longer young and
feeble—it is no longer to make an abortive struggle, and then be passive
for years: it is abroad with power—thundering at castle-gates and
prison-doors: from revolutionizing neighborhoods, it is going on to
revolutionize nations: instead of agitating a kingdom, as formerly,
it is now shaking the world. When it once fairly gets the mastery over

[1] From the *Liberator* (Boston), January 7, 1832.

its enemy Oppression, will not its retaliation be terrible? Wo to those who dress in purple and fine linen, and fare sumptuously every day, having defrauded the laborer of his hire and oppressed the poor! Wo to those who entrench themselves behind hereditary privileges and conduct, and declare that for the crimes which they commit, their ancestors must be responsible! Wo to that policy or system which has no other foundation than injustice, tyranny and wrong! which consults expediency and not right! which expects to satisfy the hungry with a crumb of knowledge—to content the benighted wanderer with a few scattered rays of light—to comfort the naked with half a blanket, or a whole suit of rags! which mocks the remonstrances of prudence, repels the suggestions of wisdom, forgets all the lessons of history, discredits the uniform results of experience, defies the moral and physical power of its victims! Wo, wo, for all that is oppressive—for all that lives by usurpation—for those who hearken not to the voice of nature —for the persecutors of their fellow men, wherever they may be found! There will be no discrimination with God or man, in favor of any class of despots: they who tread, with iron heels, upon the necks of their slaves in this country, will not be thought less blameworthy than the tyrants of Europe. Despotism in a republic is as sure of punishment, as in a monarchy.

Happy will it be for us, as a people, if, treasuring up these truths in our memories, we check the retributive thunders of justice "in mid volley," by a timely repentance. We are a nation of blind, unrelenting, haughty, cruel, heaven-daring oppressors. The chains which we rivet upon the bodies of two millions of our fellow-countrymen, are as galling and heavy as were ever forged for human limbs. Shall those chains be broken by physical or moral power? Infatuated as we may be, we are conscious that, at some period or other, in some way or other, our slaves must be free. Gigantic as may be our strength, we are too intelligent to believe that it will enable us always to oppress with impunity.

. . . So long as we continue one body—a union—a nation—the compact involves us in the guilt and danger of slavery. If the slaves, goaded to desperation by their cruel masters, should rise *en masse* to obtain redress, do the citizens of New-England reflect, that they are constitutionally bound to assist the southern taskmasters in subduing or exterminating the blacks and are liable to be drafted at a moment's warning? Perhaps we imagine, that there is little danger of a general insurrection among the slaves—(the recent events at the south to the contrary, notwithstanding)—but does this circumstance remove the responsibility from our shoulders? No matter what is the *probability* in this case. The question is, whether we are not solemnly pledged to put down a black rebellion in the south? At the present moment, indeed, appearances seem to indicate a double rebellion in that section of the Union; a rebellion against the Government by the whites, and a rebellion against the whites by the blacks; so that the "tug of war" may be nearer than the people of the free states imagine. What protects the south from instant destruction? OUR PHYSICAL FORCE. Break the chain which binds her to the Union, and the scenes of St. Domingo would be witnessed throughout her borders. She may affect to laugh at this prophecy; but she knows that her security lies in northern bayonets. Nay, she has repeatedly taunted the free states with being pledged to protect her: tyrannise long and cruelly as she may, they are bound to give her life, and, if necessary, to slaughter her slaves. How, then, do we make the inquiry, with affected astonishment, "what have we to do with the guilt of slavery?" Is this a novel view of the subject? Must we now begin to inquire, for the first time, what are our duties and responsibilities as American citizens?

Perhaps we internally resolve never to march against the blacks— never to bear arms south of the Potomac. But such a decision would be full of treachery to the people of the south. Let us give them fair warning when we intend to leave them to their fate; and let us not practise studied cruelty and deceit. Hear the language of a Representative from Massachusetts [Mr. Dwight] in the Congressional session of 1827:

> In an internal commotion in Georgia, where should its white population seek a shelter? Not, certainly, in the little fort of Savannah. In such an event, [and he hoped the day was far distant,] they would not look to the forts erected for maritime defence, but to the *stout hearts* and *sympathetic feelings* of their *northern brethren;* and he did not hazard too much in saying, that in such a case the north will *pour out its blood like water* to assist the south!

Are these indeed our sentiments? Can we cover ourselves with laurels in a war of oppression? What! ready to pour out our blood like water, in order that a large portion of our fellow countrymen may be kept in servile bondage!

It is awful to reflect, that it is solely by the authority of the free states that slavery is tolerated in our land. The south is only our agent. We form a powerful combination which cannot be resisted, and give her a broad license to kidnap, plunder and oppress; promising our united aid, in case she is in personal danger! Yet we complacently wipe our mouths, and say, "We commit no evil—the south is the victim to be sacrificed." This is certainly an improvement upon the Holy Alliance. We are guilty—all guilty—horribly guilty. . . .

5

Garrison on Colonization and Race Prejudice[1]

To promote the goal of immediate emancipation,
Garrison attacked the American Colonization Society, with its
professed aim of gradual emancipation through colonization.
The assault upon the motives and plans of the colonizationists
began with a speech in Philadelphia in 1830, but Garrison's most
sustained and thorough denunciation came in his book Thoughts
on African Colonization *(1832). In a chapter entitled "The Amer-*
ican Colonization Society Denies the Possibility of Elevating the
Blacks in this Country," Garrison reached unparalleled heights
of invective and at the same time made his fullest statement on
the problem of racial prejudice.

The detestation of feeling, the fire of moral indignation, and the
agony of soul which I have felt kindling and swelling within me, in
the progress of this review, under this section reach the acme of intensity. It is impossible for the mind to conceive, or the tongue to utter,
or the pen to record, sentiments more derogatory to the character of a
republican and christian people than the following: [Garrison then
provides several pages of excerpts from colonizationist writing, most
of it purporting to show that white prejudice is ineradicable and that
discrimination against the Negro in the United States cannot be eliminated, thus leading to the conclusion that the only hope for Negro
freedom is colonization in Africa.]

"My bowels, my bowels! I am pained at my very heart; my heart
maketh a noise in me." Are we pagans, are we savages, are we devils?
Can pagans, or savages, or devils, exhibit a more implacable spirit,
than is seen in the foregoing extracts? It is enough to cause the very
stones to cry out, and the beasts of the field to rebuke us.

[1] From William Lloyd Garrison, *Thoughts on African Colonization* (Boston, 1832),
pp. 134, 141–47, 149–50.

31

Of this I am sure: no man, who is truly willing to admit the people of color to an equality with himself, can see any insuperable difficulty in effecting their elevation. When, therefore, I hear an individual—especially a professor of christianity—strenuously contending that there can be no fellowship with them, I cannot help suspecting the sincerity of his own republicanism or piety, or thinking that the beam is in his own eye. My bible assures me that the day is coming when even the "wolf shall dwell with the lamb, and the leopard shall lie down with the kid, and the wolf and the young lion and the fatling together"; and, if this be possible, I see no cause why those of the same species —God's rational creatures—fellow countrymen, in truth, cannot dwell in harmony together.

How abominably hypocritical, how consummately despicable, how incorrigibly tyrannical must this whole nation appear in the eyes of the people of Europe!—professing to be the *friends* of the free blacks, actuated by the purest motives of benevolence toward them, desirous to make atonement for past wrongs, challenging the admiration of the world for their patriotism, philanthropy and piety—and yet (hear, O heaven! and be astonished, O earth!) shamelessly proclaiming, with a voice louder than thunder, and an aspect malignant as sin, that while their colored countrymen remain among them, they must be trampled beneath their feet, treated as inferior beings, deprived of all the invaluable privileges of freemen, separated by the brand of indelible ignominy, and debased to a level with the beasts that perish! Yea, that they may as soon change their complexion as rise from their degradation! that no device of philanthropy can benefit them here! that they constitute a class out of which *no individual can be elevated,* and below which, *none can be depressed!* that no talents however great, no piety however pure and devoted, no patriotism however ardent, no industry however great, no wealth however abundant, can raise them to a footing of equality with the whites! that "let them toil from youth to old age in the honorable pursuit of wisdom—let them store their minds with the most valuable researches of science and literature—and let them add to a highly gifted and cultivated intellect, a piety pure, undefiled, and unspotted from the world, *it is all nothing*—they would not be received into the *very lowest walks of society*—admiration of such uncommon beings would mingle with *disgust!*" Yea, that "there is a broad and impassible line of demarcation between every man who has *one drop* of African blood in his veins and every other class in the community"! Yea, that "the habits, the feelings, all the prejudices of society—prejudices which neither *refinement,* nor *argument,* nor *education,* nor RELIGION itself can subdue—mark the people of color, whether bond or free, as the subjects of a degradation *inevitable* and *incurable*"! Yea, that *"Christianity* cannot do for them here, what it will do for them in Africa"! Yea, that "this is not the fault of the colored man; NOR OF THE WHITE MAN, nor of Christianity; but AN ORDINATION OF PROVIDENCE, *and no more to be changed than the* LAWS OF NATURE" ! ! !

Again I ask, are we pagans, are we savages, are we devils? Search the records of heathenism, and sentiments more hostile to the spirit of the gospel, or of a more black and blasphemous complexion than these, cannot be found. I believe that they are libels upon the character of my countrymen, which time will wipe off. I call upon the spirits of the just made perfect in heaven, upon all who have experienced the love of God in their souls here below, upon the christian converts in India and the islands of the sea, to sustain me in the assertion that there *is* power enough in the religion of Jesus Christ to melt down the most stubborn prejudices, to overthrow the highest walls of partition, to break the strongest caste, to improve and elevate the most degraded, to unite in fellowship the most hostile, and to equalize and bless all its recipients. Make me *sure* that there is not, and I will give it up, now and for ever. "In Christ Jesus, all are one: there is neither Jew nor Greek, there is neither bond nor free, there is neither male nor female."

These sentiments were not uttered by infidels, nor by worthless wretches, but in many instances by professors of religion and *ministers of the gospel!* and in almost every instance by reputedly the most enlightened, patriotic and benevolent men in the land! Tell it not abroad! publish it not in the streets of Calcutta! Even the eminent President of Union College, (Rev. Dr. Nott,) could so far depart, unguardedly I hope, from christian love and integrity, as to utter this language in an address in behalf of the Colonization Society:—"With us they [the free people of color] have been degraded by slavery, and *still further degraded by the mockery of nominal freedom.*" Were this true, it would imply that we of the free States are more barbarous and neglectful than even the traffickers in souls and men-stealers at the south. We have not, it is certain, treated our colored brethren as the law of kindness and the ties of brotherhood demand; but have we outdone slaveholders in cruelty? Were it true, to forge new fetters for the limbs of these degraded beings would be an act of benevolence.

But their condition is as much superior to that of the slaves, as happiness is to misery. The second portion of this work, containing their proceedings in a collective capacity, shows whether they have made any progress in intelligence, in virtue, in piety, and in happiness, since their liberation. Again he says: *"We have endeavored,* but endeavored in vain, *to restore them either to self-respect, or to the respect of others."* It is painful to contradict so worthy an individual; but nothing is more certain than that this statement is altogether erroneous. We have derided, we have shunned, we have neglected them, in every possible manner. They have had to rise not only under the mountainous weight of their own ignorance and vice, but with the additional and constant pressure of our contempt and injustice. In despite of us, they have done well. Again: *"It is not our fault that we have failed;* it is not theirs."* We *are* wholly and exclusively in fault. What have we done to raise them up from the earth? What have we *not* done to keep them down? Once more: "It has resulted from a cause over which neither they, nor we, can ever have control." In other words, they have been made with skins "not colored like our own," and *therefore* we cannot recognise them as fellow-countrymen, or treat them like rational beings! One sixth of our whole population *must,* FOR EVER, in this land, remain a wretched, ignorant and degraded race,—and yet nobody be culpable—*none but the Creator* who has made us *incapable* of doing unto others as we would have them do unto us! Horrible—horrible! If this be not an impeachment of Infinite Goodness,—I do not say intentionally but *really,*—I cannot define it. The same sentiment is reiterated by a writer in the Southern Religious Telegraph, who says—"The exclusion of the free black from the civil and literary privileges of our country, depends on another circumstance than that of character—a circumstance, which, as it was entirely beyond his control, so it is unchangeable, and will for ever operate. This circumstance is—*he is a black man"* ! ! And the Board of Managers of the Parent Society, in their Fifteenth Annual Report, declare that *"an ordination of Providence"* prevents the general improvement of the people of color in this land! How are God and our country dishonored, and the requirements of the gospel contemned, by this ungodly plea! Having satisfied himself that the Creator is alone blameable for the past and present degradation of the free blacks, Dr. Nott draws the natural and unavoidable inference that "here, therefore, they must be *for ever debased, for ever useless, for ever a nuisance, for ever a calamity,"* and then gravely declares (mark the

climax!) "and yet THEY, [these ignorant, helpless, miserable creatures!]
AND THEY ONLY, are qualified for colonizing Africa"! ! "Why then,"
he asks, "*in the name of God,*"—(the abrupt appeal, in this connexion,
seems almost profane,)—"should we hesitate to encourage their departure?"

Nature, we are positively assured, has raised up impassable barriers
between the races. I understand by this expression, that the blacks are
of a different species from ourselves, so that all attempts to generate
offspring between us and them must prove as abortive, as between a
man and a beast. It is a law of Nature that the lion shall not beget
the lamb, or the leopard the bear. Now the planters at the south have
clearly demonstrated, that an amalgamation with their slaves is not
only possible, but a matter of course, and eminently productive. It
neither ends in abortion nor produces monsters. In truth, it is often
so difficult in the slave States to distinguish between the fruits of this
intercourse and the children of white parents, that witnesses are summoned at court to solve the problem! Talk of the barriers of Nature,
when the land swarms with living refutations of the statement! Happy
indeed would it be for many a female slave, if such a barrier could
exist during the period of her servitude to protect her from the lust
of her master!

In France, England, Spain, and other countries, persons of color
maintain as high a rank and are treated as honorably as any other
class of the inhabitants, in despite of the "impassable barriers of Nature." Yet it is proclaimed to the world by the Colonization Society,
that the American people can never be as republican in their feelings
and practices as Frenchmen, Spaniards or Englishmen! Nay, that *religion* itself cannot subdue their malignant prejudices, or induce them
to treat their dark-skinned brethren in accordance with their professions of republicanism! My countrymen! is it so? Are you willing thus
to be held up as tyrants and hypocrites for ever? as less magnanimous
and just than the populace of Europe? No—no! I cannot give you up
as incorrigibly wicked, nor my country as sealed over to destruction.
My confidence remains, like the oak—like the Alps—unshaken, storm-
proof. I am not discouraged—I am not distrustful. I still place an
unwavering reliance upon the omnipotence of truth. I still believe that
the demands of justice will be satisfied; that the voice of bleeding
humanity will melt the most obdurate hearts; and that the land will be
redeemed and regenerated by an enlightened and energetic public
opinion. As long as there remains among us a single copy of the

Declaration of Independence, or of the New Testament, I will not despair of the social and political elevation of my sable countrymen. Already a rallying-cry is heard from the East and the West, from the North and the South; towns and cities and states are in commotion; volunteers are trooping to the field; the spirit of freedom and the fiend of oppression are in mortal conflict, and all neutrality is at an end. Already the line of division is drawn: on one side are the friends of truth and liberty, with their banner floating high in the air, on which are inscribed in letters of light, "IMMEDIATE ABOLITION"—"NO COMPROMISE WITH OPPRESSORS"—"EQUAL RIGHTS"—"NO EXPATRIA-TION"—"DUTY, AND NOT CONSEQUENCES"—"LET JUSTICE BE DONE, THOUGH THE HEAVENS SHOULD FALL!"—On the opposite side stand the supporters and apologists of slavery in mighty array, with a black flag on which are seen in bloody characters, "AFRICAN COLONIZATION"—"GRADUAL ABOLITION"—"RIGHTS OF PROPERTY"—"POLITICAL EXPE-DIENCY"—"NO EQUALITY"—"NO REPENTANCE"—"EXPULSION OF THE BLACKS"—"PROTECTION TO TYRANTS!"—Who can doubt the issue of this controversy, or which side has the approbation of the Lord of Hosts?

In the African Repository for September, 1831, there is an elaborate defence of the Colonization Society, in which occurs the following passage:—"It has been said that the Society is unfriendly to the im-provement of the free people of color while they remain in the United States. *The charge is not true.*" I reiterate the charge; and the evidence of its correctness is before the reader. The Society prevents the educa-tion of this class in the most insidious and effectual manner, by con-stantly asserting that they must always be a degraded people in this country, and that the cultivation of their minds will avail them nothing. Who does not readily perceive that the prevalence of this opinion must at once paralyze every effort for their improvement? For it would be a waste of time and means, and unpardonable folly, for us to attempt the accomplishment of an impossible work—of that which we know will result in disappointment. Every discriminating and candid mind must see and acknowledge, that, to perpetuate their ignorance, it is only necessary to make the belief prevalent that they "must be for ever debased, for ever useless, for ever an inferior race," and their thraldom is sure. . . .

In a critical examination of the pages of the African Repository, and of the reports and addresses of the Parent Society and its auxil-iaries, I cannot find in a single instance any impeachment of the conduct and feelings of society toward the people of color, or any hint that the prejudice which is so prevalent against them is unmanly and sinful, or any evidence of contrition for past injustice, or any remonstrance or entreaty with a view to a change of public sentiment, or any symptoms of moral indignation at such unchristian and anti-republican treatment. On the contrary, I find the doctrine every where inculcated that this hatred and contempt, this abuse and proscription, are not only excusable, but the natural, inevitable and incurable effects of constitutional dissimilitude, growing out of an ordination of Providence, for which there is no remedy but a separation between the two races. If the free blacks, then, have been "still further degraded by the mockery of nominal freedom," if they "must always be a separate and degraded race," if "degradation must and will press them to the earth," if from their present station "they can never rise, be their talents, their enterprise, their virtues what they may," if "in Africa alone, they can enjoy the motives for honorable ambition," the American Colonization Society is responsible for their debasement and misery; for as it numbers among its supporters the most influential men in our country, and boasts of having the approbation of an overwhelming majority of the wise and good whose examples are laws, it is able, were it willing, to effect a radical change in public sentiment— nay, it is at the present time public sentiment itself. But though it has done much, and may do more, (all that it can it will do,) to depress, impoverish and dispirit the free people of color, and to strengthen and influence mutual antipathies, it is the purpose of God, I am fully persuaded, to humble the pride of the American people by rendering the expulsion of our colored countrymen utterly impracticable, and the necessity for their admission to equal rights imperative. As neither mountains of prejudice, nor the massy shackles of law and of public opinion, have been able to keep them down to a level with slaves, I confidently anticipate their exaltation among ourselves. Through the vista of time,—a short distance only,—I see them here, not in Africa, not bowed to the earth, or derided and persecuted as at present, not with a downcast air or an irresolute step, but standing erect as men destined heavenward, unembarrassed, untrammelled, with none to molest or make them afraid.

6

Garrison's Account of
the Broadcloth Mob[1]

*On October 21, 1835, Garrison was attacked in Boston
by an anti-abolitionist mob—one of the most dramatic of the
many incidents in which abolitionists were victims of mob violence. The mob formed because of publicity surrounding an
announced visit of George Thompson, a famous British abolitionist, to speak at a meeting of the Boston Female Anti-Slavery
Society. Shortly before the scheduled hour of the meeting, Garrison arrived at the Society's rooms on Washington Street and
found a crowd in the street—but no sign of Thompson, who, as it
turned out, never showed up. This is Garrison's own account of
the events that followed.*

As the meeting was about to commence at 3 o'clock P.M., I went
to the hall about twenty minutes before that time. Perhaps a hundred
individuals had already gathered around the street door and opposite
the building, and their number was rapidly augmenting. On ascend-
ing into the hall, I found about fifteen or twenty ladies assembled,
sitting with cheerful countenances, and a crowd of noisy intruders
(mostly young men) gazing upon them, through whom I urged my
way with considerable difficulty. "That's Garrison," was the exclama-
tion of some of these creatures, as I quietly took my seat. Perceiving
that they had no intention of retiring, I went to them and calmly said
—"Gentlemen, perhaps you are not aware that this is a meeting of the
Boston *Female* Anti-Slavery Society, called and intended exclusively
for *ladies,* and those only who have been invited to address them.
Understanding this fact, you will not be so rude or indecorous as to
thrust your presence upon this meeting. If, *gentlemen,*" I pleasantly
continued, "any of you are *ladies*—in disguise—why, only apprise me
of the fact, give me your names, and I will introduce you to the rest of

[1] From W. P. Garrison and F. J. Garrison, *Life,* II, 11–30.

your sex, and you can take seats among them accordingly." I then sat down, and, for a few moments, their conduct was more orderly. However, the stairway and upper door of the hall were soon densely filled with a brazen-faced crew, whose behavior grew more and more indecent and outrageous.

Perceiving that it would be impracticable for me, or any other person, to address the ladies; and believing, as I was the only male abolitionist in the hall, that my presence would serve as a pretext for the mob to annoy the meeting, I held a short colloquy with the excellent President of the Society, telling her that I would withdraw, unless she particularly desired me to stay. It was her earnest wish that I would retire, as well for my own safety as for the peace of the meeting. She assured me that the Society would resolutely but calmly proceed to the transaction of its business, and leave the issue with God. I left the hall accordingly, and would have left the building if the staircase had not been crowded to excess. This being impracticable, I retired into the Anti-Slavery Office, (which is separated from the hall by a board partition), accompanied by my friend Mr. Charles C. Burleigh. It was deemed prudent to lock the door, to prevent the mob from rushing in and destroying our publications.

In the meantime, the crowd in the street had augmented from a hundred to thousands. The cry was for "Thompson! Thompson!"— but the Mayor had now arrived, and, addressing the rioters, he assured them that Mr. Thompson was not in the city, and besought them to disperse. As well might he have attempted to propitiate a troop of ravenous wolves. None went away—but the tumult continued momentarily to increase. It was apparent, therefore, that the hostility of the throng was not concentrated upon Mr. Thompson, but that it was as deadly against the Society and the Anti-Slavery cause. This fact is worthy of special note—for it incontestably proves that the object of the "respectable and influential" rioters was to put down the cause of emancipation, and that Mr. Thompson furnished merely a pretext for five thousand "gentlemen" to mob thirty Christian women! . . .

Notwithstanding the presence and frantic behavior of the rioters in the hall, the meeting of the Society was regularly called to order by the President. She then read a select and an exceedingly appropriate portion of Scripture, and offered up a fervent prayer to God for direction and succor, and the forgiveness of enemies and revilers. It was an awful, sublime and soul-thrilling scene—enough, one would suppose, to melt adamantine hearts, and make even fiends of darkness stagger and retreat. Indeed, the clear, untremulous tone of voice of that Christian heroine in prayer occasionally awed the ruffians into silence, and was distinctly heard even in the midst of their hisses, threats, and curses—for they could not long silently endure the agony of conviction, and their conduct became furious. They now attempted to break down the partition, and partially succeeded—but the little band of females still maintained their ground unshrinkingly, and continued to transact their business.

An assault was now made upon the door of the office, the lower panel of which was instantly dashed to pieces. Stooping down, and glaring upon me as I sat at the desk, writing an account of the riot to a distant friend, the ruffians cried out—"There he is! That's Garrison! Out with the scoundrel!" &c., &c. Turning to Mr. Burleigh, I said—"You may as well open the door, and let them come in and do their worst." But he, with great presence of mind, went out, locked the door, put the key in his pocket, and by his admirable firmness succeeded in keeping the office safe.

Two or three constables having cleared the hall and staircase of the mob, the Mayor came in and *ordered* the ladies to desist, assuring them that he could not any longer guarantee protection if they did not take immediate advantage of the opportunity to retire from the building. Accordingly they adjourned, to meet at the house of one of their number [Mrs. Chapman's, at 11 West Street], for the completion of their business; but as they passed through the crowd they were greeted with taunts, hisses and cheers of mobocratic triumph, from "gentlemen of property and standing from all parts of the city."

Even *their* absence did not diminish the throng. Thompson was not there—the ladies were not there—but "*Garrison* is there!" was the cry. "Garrison! Garrison! We must have Garrison! Out with him! Lynch him!" These and numberless other exclamations arose from the multitude. For a moment, their attention was diverted from me to the Anti-Slavery sign ["Anti-Slavery Rooms"], and they vociferously demanded its possession. It is painful to state that the Mayor promptly complied with their demand! So agitated and alarmed had he become that, in very weakness of spirit, he ordered the sign to be hurled to the ground, and it was instantly broken into a thousand fragments by the infuriated populace. O, lamentable departure from duty—O, shameful outrage upon private property—by one who had sworn, not to destroy but to protect property—not to pander to the lawless desires of a mob, however "wealthy and respectable," but to preserve the public peace.

The act was wholly unjustifiable. The Mayor might have as lawfully surrendered me to the tender mercies of the mob, or ordered the building itself to be torn down, in order to propitiate them, as to remove that sign. Perhaps—nay, *probably*—he was actuated by kind intentions; probably he hoped that he should thereby satisfy the ravenous appetites of these human cormorants, and persuade them to retire; probably he trusted thus to extricate me from danger. But the sequel proved that he only gave a fresh stimulus to popular fury: and if he could have saved my life, or the whole city from destruction, by that single act, still he ought not to have obeyed the mandate of the mob—no indeed! He committed a public outrage in the presence of the lawless and disobedient, and thus strangely expected to procure obedience to and a respect for the law! He behaved disorderly before rebels that he might restore order among them! Mr. HENRY WILLIAMS and Mr. JOHN L. DIMMOCK also deserve severe reprehension for their forwardness in taking down the sign. The offence, under such circumstances, was very heinous. The value of the article destroyed was of no consequence; but the principle involved in its surrender and sacrifice is one upon which civil government, private property and individual liberty depend.

The sign being demolished, the cry for "Garrison!" was renewed, more loudly than ever. It was now apparent that the multitude would not disperse until I had left the building; and as egress out of the front door was impossible, the Mayor and his assistants, as well as some of my friends, earnestly besought me to effect my escape in the rear of the building. At this juncture, an abolition brother whose mind had not been previously settled on the peace question, in his anguish and alarm for my safety, and in view of the helplessness of the civil authority, said—"I must henceforth repudiate the principle of non-resistance. When the civil arm is powerless, my own rights are trodden in the dust, and the lives of my friends are put in imminent peril by ruffians, I will hereafter prepare to defend myself and them at all hazards." Putting my hand upon his shoulder, I said,

Hold, my dear brother! You know not what spirit you are of. This is the trial of our faith, and the test of our endurance. Of what value or utility are the principles of peace and forgiveness, if we may repudiate them in the hour of peril and suffering? Do you wish to become like one of those violent and bloodthirsty men who are seeking my life? Shall we give blow for blow, and array sword against sword? God forbid!

I will perish sooner than raise my hand against any man, even in self-defence, and let none of my friends resort to violence for my protection. If my life be taken, the cause of emancipation will not suffer. God reigns—his throne is undisturbed by this storm—he will make the wrath of man to praise him, and the remainder he will restrain—his omnipotence will at length be victorious.

Preceded by my faithful and beloved friend Mr. J—— R—— C——, I dropped from a back window on to a shed, and narrowly escaped falling headlong to the ground. We entered into a carpenter's shop, through which we attempted to get into Wilson's Lane, but found our retreat cut off by the mob. They raised a shout as soon as we came in sight, but the workmen promptly closed the door of the shop, kept them at bay for a time, and thus kindly afforded me an opportunity to find some other passage. I told Mr. C. it would be futile to attempt to escape—I would go out to the mob, and let them deal with me as they might elect; but he thought it was my duty to avoid them as long as possible. We then went up stairs, and, finding a vacancy in one corner of the room, I got into it, and he and a young lad piled up some boards in front of me to shield me from observation. In a few minutes several ruffians broke into the chamber, who seized Mr. C. in a rough manner, and led him out to the view of the mob, saying, "This is not Garrison, but Garrison's and Thompson's friend, and he says he knows where Garrison is, but won't tell." Then a shout of exultation was raised by the mob, and what became of him I do not know; though, as I was immediately discovered, I presume he escaped without material injury.

On seeing me, three or four of the rioters, uttering a yell, furiously dragged me to the window, with the intention of hurling me from that height to the ground; but one of them relented and said—"Don't let us kill him outright." So they drew me back, and coiled a rope about my body—probably to drag me through the streets. I bowed to the mob, and, requesting them to wait patiently until I could descend, went down upon a ladder that was raised for that purpose. I fortunately extricated myself from the rope, and was seized by two or three powerful men, to whose firmness, policy and muscular energy I am probably indebted for my preservation. They led me along bareheaded, (for I had lost my hat), through a mighty crowd, ever and anon shouting, "He shan't be hurt! You shan't hurt him! Don't hurt him! He is an American," &c., &c. This seemed to excite sympathy among many in the crowd, and they reiterated the cry, "He shan't be hurt!" I was thus conducted through Wilson's Lane into State Street, in the rear of the City Hall, over the ground that was stained with the blood of the first martyrs in the cause of LIBERTY and INDEPENDENCE, by the memorable massacre of 1770—and upon which was proudly unfurled, only a few years since, with joyous acclamations, the beautiful banner presented to the gallant Poles by the young men of Boston! What a scandalous and revolting contrast! My offence was in pleading for LIBERTY—liberty for my enslaved countrymen, colored though they be —liberty of speech and of the press for ALL! And upon that "consecrated spot" I was made an object of derision and scorn, and my body was denuded of a large portion of its covering, in the presence of thousands of my fellow citizens! O, base degeneracy from their parent-stock!

Orders were now given to carry me to the Mayor's office in the City Hall. As we approached the south door, the Mayor attempted to protect me by his presence; but as he was unassisted by any show of authority or force, he was quickly thrust aside—and now came a tremendous rush on the part of the mob to prevent my entering the Hall. For a moment, the conflict was dubious—but my sturdy supporters carried me safely up to the Mayor's room.

Whatever those newspapers which were instrumental in stirring up the mob may report, throughout the whole of this trying scene, I felt perfectly calm, nay, very happy. It seemed to me that it was indeed a blessed privilege thus to suffer in the cause of Christ. Death did not present one repulsive feature. The promises of God sustained my soul, so that it was not only divested of fear, but ready to sing aloud for joy.

Having had my clothes [it was a bran-new suit] rent asunder, one individual kindly lent me a pair of pantaloons—another, a coat—a third, a stock—a fourth, a cap as a substitute for my lost hat. After a consultation of fifteen or twenty minutes, the Mayor and his advisers came to the singular conclusion, that the building would be endangered by my continuing in it, and that the preservation of my life depended upon committing me to jail, ostensibly as a disturber of the peace! ! A hack was got in readiness at the door to receive me— and, supported by Sheriff Parkman and Ebenezer Bailey, Esq. (the mayor leading the way), I succeeded in getting into it without much difficulty, as I was not readily identified in my new garb. Now came a scene that baffles the power of description. As the ocean, lashed into fury by the spirit of the storm, seeks to whelm the adventurous bark beneath its mountain waves—so did the mob, enraged by a series of disappointments, rush like a whirlwind upon the frail vehicle in which I sat, and endeavor to drag me out of it. Escape seemed a physical impossibility. They clung to the wheels—dashed open the doors— seized hold of the horses—and tried to upset the carriage. They were, however, vigorously repulsed by the police—a constable sprang in by my side—the doors were closed—and the driver, lustily using his whip upon the bodies of his horses and the heads of the rioters, happily made an opening through the crowd, and drove at a tremendous speed for Leverett Street. But many of the rioters followed even with superior swiftness, and repeatedly attempted to arrest the progress of the horses. To reach the jail by a direct course was found impracticable; and after going in a circuitous direction, and encountering many "hair-breadth 'scapes," we drove up to this new and last refuge of liberty and life, when another bold attempt was made to seize me by the mob—but in vain. In a few moments I was locked up in a cell, safe from my perse- cutors, accompanied by two delightful associates, a good conscience and a cheerful mind. In the course of the evening, several of my friends came to my grated window to sympathise and rejoice with me, with whom I held a pleasant conversation until the hour of retirement, when I threw myself upon my prison bed, and slept tranquilly during the night. In the morning I awoke quite refreshed, and, after eating an excellent breakfast furnished by the kindness of my keeper, I inscribed upon the walls of my cell the following items:

> Wm. Lloyd Garrison was put into this cell on Wednesday afternoon, Oct. 21, 1835, to save him from the violence of a "respectable and influ- ential" mob, who sought to destroy him for preaching the abominable and dangerous doctrine, that "all men are created equal," and that all oppression is odious in the sight of God. "Hail, Columbia!" Cheers for the Autocrat of Russia and the Sultan of Turkey!
>
> Reader, let this inscription remain till the last slave in this despotic land be loosed from his fetters.

When peace within the bosom reigns,
    And conscience gives th' approving voice;
Though bound the human form in chains,
    Yet can the soul aloud rejoice.

'Tis true, my footsteps are confined—
    I cannot range beyond this cell;—

But what can circumscribe my mind?
To chain the winds attempt as well!

Confine me as a prisoner—but bind me not as a slave.
Punish me as a criminal—but hold me not as a chattel.
Torture me as a man—but drive me not like a beast.
Doubt my sanity—but acknowledge my immortality.

In the course of the forenoon, after passing through the mockery of an examination, for form's sake, before Judge Whitman, I was released from prison; but at the *earnest solicitation of the city authorities,* in order to tranquillize the public mind, I deemed it proper to leave the city for a few days, and accordingly took my departure, accompanied by Mrs. Garrison.

My thanks are due to Sheriff Parkman for various acts of politeness and kindness; as also to Sheriff Sumner, Mr. Coolidge, Mr. Andrews, and several other gentlemen.

I have been thus minute in describing the rise, progress and termination of this disgraceful riot, in order to prevent (or rather to correct) false representations and exaggerated reports respecting it and myself. It is proper to subjoin a few reflections.

1. The outrage was perpetrated in Boston—the Cradle of Liberty—the city of Hancock and Adams—the headquarters of refinement, literature, intelligence, and religion! No comments can add to the infamy of this fact.

2. It was perpetrated in the open daylight of heaven, and was therefore most unblushing and daring in its features.

3. It was against the friends of human freedom—the liberty of speech—the right of association—and in support of the vilest slavery that ever cursed the world.

4. It was dastardly beyond precedent, as it was an assault of thousands upon a small body of helpless females. Charleston and New Orleans have never acted so brutally. Courageous cravens!

5. It was planned and executed, not by the rabble, or the workingmen, but by "*gentlemen* of property and standing from all parts of the city"—and now [October 25] that time has been afforded for reflection, it is still either openly justified or coldly disapproved by the "higher classes," and exultation among them is general throughout the city. . . .

7. It is evidently winked at by the city authorities. No efforts have

been made to arrest the leading rioters. The Mayor has made no public appeal to the citizens to preserve order; nor has he given any assurance that the right of free discussion shall be enjoyed without molestation; nor did he array any military force against the mob, or attempt to disperse them except by useless persuasion; on the contrary, he complied with their wishes in tearing down the anti-slavery sign. He was chairman, too, of the pro-slavery meeting in Faneuil Hall, at which WASHINGTON was cheered for being a SLAVEHOLDER! . . .

7

Garrison Embraces Perfectionism[1]

By 1837, Garrison's reform interests had broadened, and his social philosophy had become more radical. Dissension and division in the antislavery movement were to result from his desire to combine abolition with other unpopular reforms and from his promulgation of the doctrine of "nonresistance," a form of Christian anarchism that denied the legitimacy of all human government. Perhaps the best statement of Garrison's new "perfectionism" is to be found in the following manifesto, published in the Liberator *of December 15, 1837.*

The termination of the present year will complete the seventh volume of the *Liberator*: we have served, therefore, a regular apprenticeship in the cause of LIBERTY, and are now prepared to advocate it upon a more extended scale.

In commencing this publication, we had but a single object in view —the total abolition of American slavery, and as a just consequence, the complete enfranchisement of our colored countrymen. As the first step towards this sublime result, we found the overthrow of the American Colonization Society to be indispensable,—containing, as it did, in its organization, all the elements of prejudice, caste, and slavery.

In entering upon our eighth volume, the abolition of slavery will still be the grand object of our labors, though not, perhaps, so exclusively as heretofore. There are other topics which, in our opinion, are intimately connected with the great doctrine of inalienable human rights; and which, while they conflict with no religious sect, or political party, as such, are pregnant with momentous consequences to the freedom, equality, and happiness of mankind. These we shall discuss as time and opportunity may permit.

The motto upon our banner has been, from the commencement of

[1] From the *Liberator* (Boston), December 15, 1837.

47

our moral warfare, "OUR COUNTRY IS THE WORLD—OUR COUNTRYMEN
ARE ALL MANKIND." We trust that it will be our only epitaph. Another
motto we have chosen is, UNIVERSAL EMANCIPATION. Up to this time
we have limited its application to those who are held in this country,
by Southern taskmasters, as marketable commodities, goods and chattels, and implements of husbandry. Henceforth we shall use it in its
widest latitude: the emancipation of our whole race from the dominion
of man, from the thraldom of self, from the government of brute force,
from the bondage of sin—and bringing them under the dominion of
God, the control of an inward spirit, the government of the law of
love, and into the obedience and liberty of Christ, who is *"the same,*
yesterday, TO-DAY, and forever."

It has never been our design, in conducting the *Liberator,* to require
of the friends of emancipation any political or sectarian shibboleth;
though, in consequence of the general corruption of all political parties
and religious sects, and of the obstacles which they have thrown into
the path of emancipation, we have been necessitated to reprove them
all. Nor have we any intention,—at least, not while ours professes to
be an anti-slavery publication, distinctively and eminently,—to assail
or give the preference to any sect or party. We are bound by no de-
nominational trammels; we are not political partisans; we have taken
upon our lips no human creed; we are guided by no human authority;
we cannot consent to wear the livery of any fallible body. The abolition
of American slavery we hold to be COMMON GROUND, upon which men
of all creeds, complexions and parties, if they have true humanity in
their hearts, may meet on amicable and equal terms to effect a common
object. But whoever marches on to that ground, loving his creed, or
sect, or party, or any worldly interest, or personal reputation or
property, or friends, or wife, or children, or life itself, more than the
cause of bleeding humanity,—or expecting to promote his political
designs, or to enforce his sectarian dogmas, or to drive others from the
ranks on account of their modes of faith,—will assuredly prove himself
to be unworthy of his abolition profession, and his real character will
be made manifest to all, for severe and unerring tests will be applied
frequently: it will not be possible for him to make those sacrifices, or
to endure those trials, which unbending integrity to the cause will
require. For ourselves, we care not who is found upon this broad platform of our common nature: if he will join hands with us, in good
faith, to undo the heavy burdens and break the yokes of our enslaved
countrymen, we shall not stop to inquire whether he is a Trinitarian

or Unitarian, Baptist or Methodist, Catholic or Covenanter, Presbyterian or Quaker, Swedenborgian or Perfectionist. However widely we may differ in our views on other subjects, we shall not refuse to labor with him against slavery, in the same phalanx, if he refuse not to labor with us. Certainly no man can truly affirm that we have sought to bring any other religious or political tests into this philanthropic enterprise than these:—"Thou shalt love thy neighbor as thyself"—"Whatsoever ye would that men should do to you, do ye even so to them"—"Remember those in bonds as bound with them." . . .

Next to the overthrow of slavery, the cause of PEACE will command our attention. The doctrine of non-resistance as commonly received and practised by Friends, and certain members of other religious denominations, we conceive to be utterly indefensible in its application to national wars:—not that it "goes too far," but that it does not go far enough. If a nation may not redress its wrongs by physical force— if it may not repel or punish a foreign enemy who comes to plunder, enslave or murder its inhabitants—then it may not resort to arms to quell an insurrection, or send to prison or suspend upon a gibbet any transgressors upon its soil. If the slaves of the South have not an undoubted right to resist their masters in the last resort, then no man, or body of men, may appeal to the law of violence in self-defence—for none have ever suffered, or can suffer, more than they. If, when men are robbed of their earnings, their liberties, their personal ownership, their wives and children, they may not resist, in no case can physical resistance be allowable, either in an individual or collective capacity.

Now the doctrine we shall endeavor to inculcate is, that the kingdoms of this world are to become the kingdoms of our Lord and of his Christ; consequently, that they are all to be supplanted, whether they are called despotic, monarchical, or republican, and he only who is King of kings, and Lord of lords, is to rule in righteousness. The kingdom of God is to be established IN ALL THE EARTH, and it shall never be destroyed, but it shall "BREAK IN PIECES AND CONSUME ALL OTHERS": its elements are righteousness and peace, and joy in the Holy Ghost: without are dogs, and sorcerers, and whoremongers, and murderers, and idolators, and whatsoever loveth and maketh a lie. Its government is one of love, not of military coercion or physical restraint: its laws are not written upon parchment, but upon the hearts of its subjects—they are not conceived in the wisdom of man, but framed by the Spirit of God: its weapons are not carnal, but spiritual. Its soldiers are clad in the whole armor of God, having their loins girt about with truth, and having on the breastplate of righteousness; their feet are shod with the preparation of the gospel of peace; with the shield of faith they are able to quench all the fiery darts of the wicked, and they wear the helmet of salvation, and wield the sword of the Spirit, which is the word of God. Hence, when smitten on the one cheek, they turn the other also; being defamed, they entreat; being reviled, they bless; being persecuted, they suffer it; they take joyfully the spoiling of their goods; they rejoice, inasmuch as they are partakers of Christ's sufferings; they are sheep in the midst of wolves; in no extremity whatever, even if their enemies are determined to nail them to the cross with Jesus, and if they, like him, could summon legions of angels to their rescue, will they resort to the law of violence.

As to the governments of this world, whatever their titles or forms, we shall endeavor to prove that, in their essential elements, and as at present administered, they are all Anti-Christ; that they can never, by human wisdom, be brought into conformity to the will of God; that they cannot be maintained except by naval and military power; that all their penal enactments, being a dead letter without an army to carry them into effect, are virtually written in human blood; and that the followers of Jesus should instinctively shun their stations of honor, power, and emolument—at the same time "submitting to every ordinance of man, for the Lord's sake," and offering no *physical* resistance to any of their mandates, however unjust or tyrannical. The language of Jesus is, "My kingdom is not of this world, else would my servants fight." Calling his disciples to him, he said to them, "Ye know that they which are accustomed to rule over the Gentiles, exercise lordship over them; and their great ones exercise authority upon them. *But so it* SHALL NOT *be among* YOU; but whosoever will be great among you, shall be your minister; and whosoever of you will be the chiefest, shall be servant of all. For even the Son of man came not to be ministered unto, but to minister, and to give his life a ransom for many."

Human governments are to be viewed as judicial punishments. If a people turn the grace of God into lasciviousness, or make their liberty an occasion for anarchy,—or if they refuse to belong to the "one fold and one Shepherd,"—they shall be scourged by governments of their own choosing, and burdened with taxation, and subjected to physical control, and torn by factions, and made to eat the fruit of their evil doings, until they are prepared to receive the liberty and the rest which remain, on earth as well as in heaven, for THE PEOPLE OF GOD. This is in strict accordance with the arrangement of Divine Providence.

So long as men contemn the perfect government of the Most High, and will not fill up the measure of Christ's sufferings in their own persons, just so long will they desire to usurp authority over each other—just so long will they pertinaciously cling to human governments, *fashioned in the likeness and administered in the spirit of their own disobedience.* Now, if the prayer of our Lord be not a mockery; if the Kingdom of God is to come universally, and his will to be done ON EARTH AS IT IS IN HEAVEN; and if, in that kingdom, no carnal weapon can be wielded, and swords are beaten into ploughshares, and spears into pruning-hooks, and there is none to molest or make afraid, and no statute-book but the Bible, and no judge but Christ; then why are not Christians obligated to come out NOW, and be separate from "the kingdoms of this world," which are all based upon THE PRINCIPLE OF VIOLENCE, and which require their officers and servants to govern and be governed by that principle? . . .

These are among the views we shall offer in connection with the heaven-originated cause of PEACE,—views which any person is at liberty to controvert in our columns, and for which no man or body of men is responsible but ourselves. If any man shall affirm that the anti-slavery cause, as such, or any anti-slavery society, is answerable for our sentiments on this subject, to him may be justly applied the apostolic declaration, "the truth is not in him." We regret, indeed, that the principles of abolitionists seem to be quite unsettled upon a question of such vast importance, and so vitally connected with the bloodless overthrow of slavery. It is time for all our friends to know where they stand. If those whose yokes they are endeavoring to break by the fire and hammer of God's word, would not, in their opinion, be justified in appealing to physical force, how can they justify others of a different complexion in doing the same thing? And if they conscientiously believe that the slaves would be guiltless in shedding the blood of their merciless oppressors, let them say so unequivocally—for there is no neutral ground in this matter, and the time is near when they will be compelled to take sides.

As our object is *universal* emancipation,—to redeem woman as well as man from a servile to an equal condition,—we shall go for the RIGHTS OF WOMAN to their utmost extent.

8

"No Union with Slaveholders" (1844)[1]

Garrison's belief that the Constitution was a proslavery compact and that consequently the Union should be dissolved became the official position of the American Anti-Slavery Society in 1844. This action was not surprising, because Garrison and his followers had seized control of the society in 1840, forcing the moderate abolitionists to withdraw and form another antislavery organization. The following statement in favor of Northern secession was written by Garrison, approved by the Anti-Slavery Society, and printed in the Liberator *for May 31, 1844.*

ADDRESS TO THE FRIENDS OF FREEDOM AND EMANCIPATION IN THE UNITED STATES

At the Tenth Anniversary of the American Anti-Slavery Society, held in the city of New-York, May 7th, 1844,—after grave deliberation, and a long and earnest discussion,—it was decided, by a vote of nearly three to one of the members present, that fidelity to the cause of human freedom, hatred of oppression, sympathy for those who are held in chains and slavery in this republic, and allegiance to God, require that the existing national compact should be instantly dissolved; that secession from the government is a religious and political duty; that the motto inscribed on the banner of Freedom should be, NO UNION WITH SLAVEHOLDERS; that it is impracticable for tyrants and the enemies of tyranny to coalesce and legislate together for the preservation of human rights, or the promotion of the interests of Liberty; and that revolutionary ground should be occupied by all those who abhor the thought of doing evil that good may come, and who do not mean to compromise the principles of Justice and Humanity.

. . . It matters not what is the theory of the government, if the

[1] From the *Liberator* (Boston), May 31, 1844.

practice of the government be unjust and tyrannical. We rise in rebellion against a despotism incomparably more dreadful than that which induced the colonists to take up arms against the mother country; not on account of a three-penny tax on tea, but because fetters of living iron are fastened on the limbs of millions of our countrymen, and our most sacred rights are trampled in the dust. As citizens of the State, we appeal to the State in vain for protection and redress. As citizens of the United States, we are treated as outlaws in one half of the country, and the national government consents to our destruction. We are denied the right of locomotion, freedom of speech, the right of petition, the liberty of the press, the right peaceably to assemble together to protest against oppression and plead for liberty—at least in thirteen States of the Union. If we venture, as avowed and unflinching abolitionists, to travel South of Mason and Dixon's line, we do so at the peril of our lives. If we would escape torture and death, on visiting any of the slave States, we must stifle our conscientious convictions, bear no testimony against cruelty and tyranny, suppress the struggling emotions of humanity, divest ourselves of all letters and papers of an anti-slavery character, and do homage to the slaveholding power—or run the risk of a cruel martyrdom! These are appalling and undeniable facts.

Three millions of the American people are crushed under the American Union! They are held as slaves—trafficked as merchandize—registered as goods and chattels! The government gives them no protection—the government is their enemy—the government keeps them in chains! There they lie bleeding—we are prostrate by their side—in their sorrows and sufferings we participate—their stripes are inflicted on our bodies, their shackles are fastened on our limbs, their cause is ours! The Union which grinds them to the dust rests upon us, and with them we will struggle to overthrow it! The Constitution which subjects them to hopeless bondage, is one that we cannot swear to support! Our motto is, "NO UNION WITH SLAVEHOLDERS," either religious or political. They are the fiercest enemies of mankind, and the bitterest foes of God! We separate from them not in anger, not in malice, not for a selfish purpose, not to do them an injury, not to cease warning, exhorting, reproving them for their crimes, not to leave the perishing bondman to his fate—O no! But to clear our skirts of innocent blood—to give the oppressor no countenance—to signify our abhorrence of injustice and cruelty—to testify against an ungodly compact—to cease striking hands with thieves and consenting with adulterers—to make no compromise with tyranny—to walk worthily of our high profession—to increase our moral power over the nation —to obey God and vindicate the gospel of his Son—to hasten the downfall of slavery in America, and throughout the world!

We are not acting under a blind impulse. We have carefully counted the cost of this warfare, and are prepared to meet its consequences. It will subject us to reproach, persecution, infamy—it will prove a fiery ordeal to all who shall pass through it—it may cost us our lives. We shall be ridiculed as fools, scorned as visionaries, branded as dis-organizers, reviled as madmen, threatened and perhaps punished as traitors. But we shall bide our time. Whether safety or peril, whether victory or defeat, whether life or death be ours, believing that our feet are planted on an eternal foundation, that our position is sublime and glorious, that our faith in God is rational and steadfast, that we have exceeding great and precious promises on which to rely, THAT WE ARE IN THE RIGHT, we shall not falter nor be dismayed, "though the earth be removed, and though the mountains be carried into the midst of the sea"—though our ranks be thinned to the number of "three hundred men." Freemen! are you ready for the conflict? Come what may, will you sever the chains that bind you to a slaveholding government, and declare your independence? Up, then, with the banner of revolution! Not to shed blood—not to injure the person or estate of any oppressor—not by force and arms to resist any law—not to countenance a servile insurrection—not to wield any carnal weapons! No— ours must be a bloodless strife, excepting *our* blood be shed—for we aim, as did Christ our leader, not to destroy men's lives, but to save them—to overcome evil with good—to conquer through suffering for righteousness' sake—to set the captive free by the potency of truth!

Secede, then, from the government. Submit to its exactions, but pay it no allegiance, and give it no voluntary aid. Fill no offices under it. Send no Senators or Representatives to the national or State Legislature; for what you cannot conscientiously perform yourself, you cannot ask another to perform as your agent. Circulate a declaration of DIS-UNION FROM SLAVEHOLDERS, throughout the country. Hold mass meetings—assemble in Conventions—nail your banners to the mast! . . .

The form of government that shall succeed the present government of the United States, let time determine. It would be a waste of time to argue that question, until the people are regenerated and turned from their iniquity. Ours is no anarchical movement, but one of order and obedience. In ceasing from oppression, we establish liberty. What is now fragmentary, shall in due time be crystallized, and shine like a gem set in the heavens, for a light to all coming ages.

Finally—we believe that the effect of this movement will be—

First, to create discussion and agitation throughout the North; and these will lead to a general perception of its grandeur and importance.

Secondly, to convulse the slumbering South like an earthquake, and convince her that her only alternative is, to abolish slavery, or be abandoned by that power on which she now relies for safety.

Thirdly, to attack the slave power in its most vulnerable point, and to carry the battle to the gate.

Fourthly, to exalt the moral sense, increase the moral power, and invigorate the moral constitution of all who heartily espouse it.

We reverently believe that, in withdrawing from the American Union, we have the God of justice with us. We know that we have our enslaved countrymen with us. We are confident that all free hearts will be with us. We are certain that tyrants and their abettors will be against us.

In behalf of the Executive Committee of the American Anti-Slavery Society, WM. LLOYD GARRISON, *President*

WENDELL PHILLIPS }
MARIA WESTON CHAPMAN } *Secretaries*

Boston, May 20, 1844

9

Garrison on
Uncle Tom's Cabin[1]

Garrison's review of Harriet Beecher Stowe's Uncle Tom's Cabin *in the* Liberator *of March 26, 1852, is a further indication of his soul-searching on the question of slave resistance. Here he attacks applying the doctrine of "nonresistance" to blacks only.*

In the execution of her very difficult task, Mrs. Stowe has displayed rare descriptive powers, a familiar acquaintance with slavery under its best and its worst phases, uncommon moral and philosophical acumen, great facility of thought and expression, feelings and emotions of the strongest character. Intimate as we have been, for a score of years, with the features and operations of the slave system, and often as we have listened to the recitals of its horrors from the lips of the poor hunted fugitives, we confess to the frequent moistening of our eyes, and the making of our heart grow liquid as water, and the trembling of every nerve within us, in the perusal of the incidents and scenes so vividly depicted in her pages. The effect of such a work upon all intelligent and humane minds coming in contact with it, and especially upon the rising generation in its plastic condition, to awaken the strongest compassion for the oppressed and the utmost abhorrence of the system which grinds them to the dust, cannot be estimated: it must be prodigious, and therefore eminently serviceable in the tremendous conflict now waged for the immediate and entire suppression of slavery on the American soil.

The appalling liabilities which constantly impend over such slaves as have "kind and indulgent masters," are thrillingly illustrated in various personal narratives; especially in that of "Uncle Tom," over whose fate every reader will drop the scalding tear, and for whose

---

[1] From the *Liberator* (Boston), March 26, 1852.

56

character the highest reverence will be felt. No insult, no outrage, no suffering, could ruffle the Christlike meekness of his spirit, or shake the steadfastness of his faith. Towards his merciless oppressors he cherished no animosity, and breathed nothing of retaliation. Like his Lord and Master, he was willing to be "led as a lamb to the slaughter," returning blessing for cursing, and anxious only for the salvation of his enemies. His character is sketched with great power and rare religious perception. It triumphantly exemplifies the nature, tendency, and results of CHRISTIAN NON-RESISTANCE.

We are curious to know whether Mrs. Stowe is a believer in the duty of non-resistance for the white man, under all possible outrage and peril, as well as for the black man; whether she is for self-defence on her own part, or that of her husband or friends or country, in case of malignant assault, or whether she impartially disarms all mankind in the name of Christ, be the danger or suffering what it may. We are curious to know this, because our opinion of her, as a religious teacher, would be greatly strengthened or lessened as the inquiry might terminate. That all the slaves of the South ought, "if smitten on the one cheek, to turn the other also,"—to repudiate all carnal weapons, shed no blood, "be obedient to their masters," wait for a peaceful deliverance, and abstain from all insurrectionary movements—is everywhere taken for granted, because the VICTIMS ARE BLACK. *They* cannot be animated by a Christian spirit and yet return blow for blow, or conspire for the destruction of their oppressors. *They* are required by the Bible to put away all wrath, to submit to every conceivable outrage without resistance, to suffer with Christ if they would reign with him. None of *their* advocates may seek to inspire *them* to imitate the example of the Greeks, the Poles, the Hungarians, our Revolutionary sires; for such teaching would evince a most unchristian and bloodthirsty disposition. For *them* there is no hope of heaven unless *they* give the most literal interpretations to the non-resisting injunctions contained in the Sermon on the Mount, touching the treatment of enemies. It is for *them*, though despoiled of all their rights and deprived of all protection, to "threaten not, but to commit the keeping of their souls to God in well-doing, as unto a faithful Creator."

Nothing can be plainer than that such conduct is obligatory upon *them;* and when, through the operations of divine grace, they are enabled to manifest a spirit like this, it is acknowledged to be worthy of great commendation, as in the case of "Uncle Tom." But, for those whose skin is of a different complexion, the case is materially altered.

When they are spit upon and buffeted, outraged and oppressed, talk not then of a non-resisting Saviour—it is fanaticism! Talk not of overcoming evil with good—it is madness! Talk not of peacefully submitting to chains and stripes—it is base servility! Talk not of servants being obedient to their masters—let the blood of the tyrants flow! How is this to be explained or reconciled? Is there one law of submission and non-resistance for the black man, and another law of rebellion and conflict for the white man? When it is the whites who are trodden in the dust, does Christ justify them in taking up arms to vindicate their rights? And when it is the blacks who are thus treated, does Christ require them to be patient, harmless, long-suffering, and forgiving? And are there two Christs?

The work, toward its conclusion, contains some objectionable sentiments respecting African colonization, which we regret to see.

10

On John Brown's Raid (1859)[1]

The greatest challenge to Garrison's peace principles came when John Brown attempted to extirpate slavery by force. The following effort to justify John Brown without completely giving up the ideal of nonresistance deserves close attention from students of antislavery ideology.

A word or two in regard to the characteristics of John Brown. He was of the old Puritan stock—a Cromwellian who "believed in God," and at the same time "in keeping his powder dry." He believed in "the sword of the Lord and of Gideon," and acted accordingly. Herein I differed widely from him. But, certainly, he was no "infidel" —oh, no! How it would have added to the fiendish malignity of the New York *Observer,* if John Brown had only been an "infidel," evangelically speaking! But being exactly of the *Observer* pattern of theology, that fact has been a very hard pill to swallow; yet, so bent upon sustaining slavery in our land is that wicked journal, that it is pre-eminently ferocious in its spirit toward John Brown, and has been loudly clamorous for his execution, notwithstanding his religious faith.

As it respects his object at Harper's Ferry, it has been truly stated here by those who have preceded me, and by John Brown himself, whose declarations to the court have been read. The man who brands him as a traitor is a calumniator. (Applause.) The man who says that his object was to promote murder, or insurrection, or rebellion, is, in the language of the apostle, "a liar, and the truth is not in him." (Loud applause.) John Brown meant to effect, if possible, a peaceful exodus from Virginia; and had not his large humanity overpowered his judgment in regard to his prisoners, he would in all probability have succeeded, and not a drop of blood would have been shed. But it is asked, "Did he not have stored up a large supply of Sharp's rifles and spears?

[1] From Garrison's speech on the evening of John Brown's execution, as printed in the *Liberator* (Boston), December 16, 1859.

What did they mean?" Nothing offensive, nothing aggressive. Only this:—he designed getting as many slaves as he could to join him, and then putting into their hands those instruments for self-defence. But, mark you! self-defence, not in standing their ground, but on their retreat to the mountains; on their flight to Canada; not with any design or wish to shed the blood or harm the hair of a single slaveholder in the State of Virginia, if a conflict could be avoided. Remember that he had the whole town in his possession for thirty-six hours; and if he had been the man so basely represented in certain quarters, he might have consummated any thing in the way of violence and blood. But, all the while, he was counselling the strictest self-defence, and forbearance to the utmost, even when he had his enemies completely in his power.

As to his trial, I affirm that it was an awful mockery, before heaven and earth! He was not tried in a court of JUSTICE. Mark how they crowded the counts together in one indictment—MURDER, TREASON, and INSURRECTION! Of what was John Brown convicted? Who knows? Perhaps some of the jury convicted him of treason; others of murder; and others, again, of insurrection. Who can tell? There was no trial on any specific point. John Brown has been judicially assassinated. It was the trial of the lamb by the wolf—nothing less. . . .

Was John Brown justified in his attempt? Yes, if Washington was in his; if Warren and Hancock were in theirs. If men are justified in striking a blow for freedom, when the question is one of a threepenny tax on tea, then, I say, they are a thousand times more justified, when it is to save fathers, mothers, wives and children from the slave-coffle and the auction-block, and to restore to them their God-given rights. (Loud applause.) Was John Brown justified in interfering in behalf of the slave population of Virginia, to secure their freedom and independence? Yes, if LaFayette was justified in interfering to help our revolutionary fathers. If Kosciusko, if Pulaski, if Steuben, if De Kalb, if all who joined them from abroad were justified in that act, then John Brown was incomparably more so. If you believe in the right of assisting men to fight for freedom who are of your own color—(God knows nothing of color or complexion—human rights know nothing of these distinctions)—then you must cover, not only with a mantle of charity, but with the admiration of your hearts, the effort of John Brown at Harper's Ferry.

I am trying him by the American standard; and I hesitate not to say, with all deliberation, that those who are attempting to decry him are dangerous members of the community; they are those in whom the love of liberty has died out; they are the lineal descendants of the tories of the Revolution, only a great deal worse. (Applause.) If the spirit of '76 prevailed to-day, as it did at that period, it would make the soil of the Commonwealth too hot to hold them. (Loud applause.) See the consistency, the vigilance, the determination of the South in support of her slave system! She moves and acts as by one impulse. Every man on her soil who is suspected of cherishing the principles of liberty is tabooed, persecuted, and brutally outraged, especially if he be from the North. She makes clean work of it, and is consistent. On the other hand, how is it at the North? Presses which are venomously pro-slavery in spirit, and wholly Southern in their design, are every where allowed; presses which insult the good name and fame of the old Commonwealth, dishonor her illustrious dead, and contemn her glorious memories, for the purpose of "crushing out" the spirit of freedom, and making absolute the sway of a ferocious slave oligarchy— and this they do with impunity. Now I say that if the North should, in defence of her free institutions, imitate the example of the South in support of slavery, there would be a speedy and thorough cleaning out of our cities and towns, of those who are desecrating the ground upon which they stand. (Loud applause.) And it would be a more hopeful state of things than it is now; for this toleration is not the result of principle, but the lack of it—it is not a noble forbearance, but a loss of vital regard for the cause of liberty.

A word upon the subject of Peace. I am a non-resistant—a believer in the inviolability of human life, under all circumstances; I, there-fore, in the name of God, disarm John Brown, and every slave at the South. But I do not stop there; if I did, I should be a monster. I also disarm, in the name of God, every slaveholder and tyrant in the world. (Loud applause.) For wherever that principle is adopted, all fetters must instantly melt, and there can be no oppressed, and no oppressor, in the nature of things. How many agree with me in regard to the doctrine of the inviolability of human life? How many non-resistants are there here to-night? (A single voice—"I.") There is *one!* (Laughter.) Well, then, you who are otherwise are not the men to point the finger at John Brown, and cry "traitor"—judging you by your own standard. (Applause.) Nevertheless, I am a non-resistant and I not only desire, but have labored unremittingly to effect, the peaceful abolition of slavery, by an appeal to the reason and conscience of the slaveholder; yet, as a peace man—an "ultra" peace man—I am prepared to say,

"Success to every slave insurrection at the South, and in every slave country." (Enthusiastic applause.) And I do not see how I compromise or stain my peace profession in making that declaration. Whenever there is a contest between the oppressed and the oppressor,—the weapons being equal between the parties,—God knows my heart must be with the oppressed, and always against the oppressor. Therefore, whenever commenced, I cannot but wish success to all slave insurrections. (Loud applause.) I thank God when men who believe in the right and duty of wielding carnal weapons are so far advanced that they will take those weapons out of the scale of despotism, and throw them into the scale of freedom. It is an indication of progress, and a positive moral growth; it is one way to get up to the sublime platform of non-resistance; and it is God's method of dealing retribution upon the head of the tyrant. Rather than see men wear their chains in a cowardly and servile spirit, I would, as an advocate of peace, much rather see them breaking the head of the tyrant with their chains. Give me, as a non-resistant, Bunker Hill, and Lexington, and Concord, rather than the cowardice and servility of a Southern slave plantation.

11
Garrison Endorses
the War (1862)[1]

After the firing on Fort Sumter, Garrison, along with most other abolitionists, endorsed the war for the Union as an act of Providence to destroy slavery. But his general support of the war was accompanied, at least until the issuance of the Emancipation Proclamation, by criticism of the government for moving too slowly against the South's "peculiar institution." Garrison was more charitable toward the administration, however, than was a group of abolitionists led by Wendell Phillips, who had a deep distrust of Lincoln. When the Emancipation Proclamation was issued, Garrison greeted it wholeheartedly and maintained that his purpose was essentially accomplished. Phillips and his followers did not agree, and thus the basis was laid for a split in the American Anti-Slavery Society. The following extracts are from Garrison's speeches of 1862.

Well, ladies and gentlemen, you remember what *Benedick* in the play says: "When I said I would die a bachelor, I did not think I should live till I were married." And when I said I would not sustain the Constitution because it was "a covenant with death and an agreement with hell," *I had no idea that I should live to see death and hell secede*. Hence it is that I am now with the Government, to enable it to constitutionally stop the further ravages of death, and to extinguish the flames of hell forever.

*   *   *

Slavery is a thunderbolt in the hands of the traitors to smite the Government to the dust. That thunderbolt might be seized and turned against the rebellion with fatal effect, and at the same time without injury to the South. My heart glows when I think of the good thus to

[1] From W. P. Garrison and F. J. Garrison, *Life*, IV, 40–45.

be done to the oppressors as well as to the oppressed; for I could not stand here, I could not stand anywhere, and advocate vindictive and destructive measures to bring the rebels to terms. I do not believe in killing or doing injury even to enemies—God forbid! That is not my Christian philosophy. But I do say, that never before in the history of the world has God vouchsafed to a Government the power to do such a work of philanthropy and justice, in the extremity of its danger and for self-preservation, as He now grants to this Government. Emancipation is to destroy nothing but evil; it is to establish good; it is to transform human beings from things into men; it is to make freedom, and education, and invention, and enterprise, and prosperity, and peace, and a true Union possible and sure. Redeemed from the curse of slavery, the South shall in due time be as the garden of God. Though driven to the wall and reduced to great extremity by this rebellion, still we hold off, hold off, hold off, and reluctantly say, at last, if it must be so, but only to save ourselves from destruction, we will do this rebellious South the most beneficent act that any people ever yet did—one that will secure historic renown for the Administration, make this struggle memorable in all ages, and bring down upon the land the benediction of God! But we will not do this if we can possibly avoid it! Now, for myself, both as an act of justice to the oppressed and to serve the cause of freedom universally, I want the Government to be in haste to blow the trump of jubilee. I desire to bless and not curse the South—to make her prosperous and happy by substituting free institutions for her leprous system of slavery. I am as much interested in the safety and welfare of the slaveholders, as brother men, as I am in the liberation of their poor slaves; for we are all the children of God, and should strive to promote the happiness of all. I desire that the mission of Jesus, "Peace on earth, good will to men," may be fulfilled in this and in every land.

*   *   *

What have we to rejoice over? Why, I say, the war! "What! this fratricidal war? What! this civil war? What! this treasonable dismemberment of the Union?" Yes, thank God for it all!—for it indicates the waning power of slavery and the irresistible growth of freedom, and that the day of Northern submission is past. It is better that we should be so virtuous that the vicious cannot live with us, than to be so vile that they can endure and relish our company. No matter what may be said of the Government—how it timidly holds back—how it lacks courage, energy, and faith—how it refuses to strike the blow which alone will settle the rebellion. No matter what may be said of President Lincoln or General McClellan, by way of criticism—and a great deal can be justly said to their condemnation—one cheering fact overrides all these considerations, making them as dust in the balance, and that is, that our free North is utterly unendurable to the slaveholding South; that we have at last so far advanced in our love of liberty and sympathy for the oppressed, as a people, that it is not possible any longer for the "traffickers in slaves and souls of men" to walk in union with us. I call that a very cheering fact. Yes, the Union is divided; but better division than that we should be under the lash of Southern overseers! Better civil war, if it must come, than for us to crouch in the dust, and allow ourselves to be driven to the wall by a miserable and merciless slave oligarchy! This war has come because of the increasing love of liberty here at the North; and although, as a people, we do not yet come up to the high standard of duty in striking directly at the slave system for its extirpation as the root and source of all our woe— nevertheless, the sentiment of the North is deepening daily in the right direction.

I hold that it is not wise for us to be too microscopic in endeavoring to find disagreeable and annoying things, still less to assume that everything is waxing worse and worse, and that there is little or no hope. No! broaden your views; take a more philosophical grasp of the great question; and see that, criticise and condemn as you may and should in certain directions, the fountains of the great deep are broken up—see that this is fundamentally a struggle between all the elements of freedom on the one hand, and all the elements of despotism on the other, with whatever of alloy in the mixture.

I repeat, the war furnishes ground for high encouragement. "Why," some may exclaim, "we thought you were a peace man!" Yes, verily, I am, and none the less so because of these declarations. Would the cause of peace be the gainer by the substitution of the power of the rebel traitors over the nation for the supremacy of the democratic idea? Would the cause of peace be promoted by the North basely yielding up all her rights and allowing her free institutions to be overthrown? Certainly not. Then, as a peace man, I rejoice that the issue is at last made up, and that the struggle is going on, because I see in it the sign of ultimate redemption. . . .

I do not know that some margin of allowance may not be made even for the Administration. I would rather be over-magnanimous than wanting in justice. Supposing Mr. Lincoln could answer to-night, and we should say to him: "Sir, with the power in your hands, slavery being the cause of the rebellion beyond all controversy, why don't you put the trump of jubilee to your lips, and proclaim universal freedom?" —possibly he might answer: "Gentlemen, I understand this matter quite as well as you do. I do not know that I differ in opinion from you; but will you insure me the support of a united North if I do as you bid me? Are all parties and all sects at the North so convinced and so united on this point that they will stand by the Government? If so, give me the evidence of it, and I will strike the blow. But, gentlemen, looking over the entire North, and seeing in all your towns and cities papers representing a considerable, if not a formidable portion of the people, menacing and bullying the Government in case it dare to liberate the slaves, even as a matter of self-preservation, I do not feel that the hour has yet come that will render it safe for the Government to take that step." I am willing to believe that something of this feeling weighs in the mind of the President and the Cabinet, and that there is some ground for hesitancy, as a mere matter of political expediency. My reply, however, to the President would be: "Sir, the power is in your hands as President of the United States, and Commander-in-Chief of the army and navy. Do *your* duty; give to the slaves their liberty by proclamation, as far as that can give it; and if the North shall betray you, and prefer the success of the rebellion to the preservation of the Union, let the dread responsibility be hers, but stand with God and Freedom on your side, come what may!" But men high in office are not apt to be led by such lofty moral considerations; and, therefore, we should not judge the present incumbents too harshly. Doubtless, they want to be assured of the Northern heart, feeling, coöperation, approval. Can these be safely relied upon when the decisive blow shall be struck? That is the question, and it is a very serious question. . . .

Nevertheless, I think the Administration is unnecessarily timid and not undeserving of rebuke. I think that this bellowing, bullying, treasonable party at the North has, after all, but very little left, either in point of numbers or power; the fangs of the viper are drawn, though the venomous feeling remains. Still, it has its effect, and produces a damaging, if not paralyzing, impression at Washington.

12

The Valedictory of the Liberator (December 29, 1865)[1]

In the last issue of the Liberator, *Garrison summed up his antislavery career.*

The present number of the *Liberator* is the completion of its thirty-fifth volume, and the termination of its existence.

Commencing my editorial career when only twenty years of age, I have followed it continuously till I have attained my sixtieth year—first, in connection with the *Free Press,* in Newburyport, in the spring of 1826; next, with the *National Philanthropist,* in Boston, in 1827; next, with the *Journal of the Times,* in Bennington, Vt., in 1828–9; next, with the *Genius of Universal Emancipation,* in Baltimore, in 1829–30; and, finally, with the *Liberator,* in Boston, from the 1st of January, 1831, to the 1st of January, 1866;—at the start, probably the youngest member of the editorial fraternity in the land, now, perhaps, the oldest, not in years, but in continuous service,—unless Mr. Bryant, of the New York *Evening Post,* be an exception.

Whether I shall again be connected with the press, in a similar capacity, is quite problematical; but, at my period of life, I feel no prompting to start a new journal at my own risk, and with the certainty of struggling against wind and tide, as I have done in the past.

I began the publication of the *Liberator* without a subscriber, and I end it—it gives me unalloyed satisfaction to say—without a farthing as the pecuniary result of the patronage extended to it during thirty-five years of unremitted labors.

From the immense change wrought in the national feeling and sentiment on the subject of slavery, the *Liberator* derived no advantage at any time in regard to its circulation. The original "disturber of the peace," nothing was left undone at the beginning, and up to the hour

[1] From the *Liberator* (Boston), December 29, 1865.

of the late rebellion, by Southern slaveholding villany on the one hand, and Northern pro-slavery malice on the other, to represent it as too vile a sheet to be countenanced by any claiming to be Christian or patriotic; and it always required rare moral courage or singular personal independence to be among its patrons. Never had a journal to look such opposition in the face—never was one so constantly belied and caricatured. If it had advocated all the crimes forbidden by the moral law of God and the statutes of the State, instead of vindicating the sacred claims of oppressed and bleeding humanity, it could not have been more vehemently denounced or more indignantly repudiated. To this day—such is the force of prejudice—there are multitudes who cannot be induced to read a single number of it, even on the score of curiosity, though their views on the slavery question are now precisely those which it has uniformly advocated. Yet no journal has been conducted with such fairness and impartiality; none has granted such freedom in its columns to its opponents; none has so scrupulously and uniformly presented all sides of every question discussed in its pages; none has so readily and exhaustively published, without note or comment, what its enemies have said to its disparagement and the vilification of its editor; none has vindicated primitive Christianity, in its spirit and purpose—"the higher law," in its supremacy over nations and governments as well as individual conscience—the Golden Rule, in its binding obligation upon all classes—the Declaration of Independence, with its self-evident truths—the rights of human nature, without distinction of race, complexion, or sex—more earnestly or more uncompromisingly; none has exerted a higher moral or more broadly reformatory influence upon those who have given it a careful perusal; and none has gone beyond it in asserting the Fatherhood of God and the brotherhood of man. All this may be claimed for it without egotism or presumption. It has ever been "a terror to evil-doers, and a praise to them that do well." It has excited the fierce hostility of all that is vile and demoniacal in the land, and won the affection and regard of the purest and noblest of the age. To me it has been unspeakably cheering, and the richest compensation for whatever of peril, suffering, and defamation I have been called to encounter, that one uniform testimony has been borne, by those who have had its weekly perusal, as to the elevating and quickening influence of the *Liberator* upon their character and lives; and the deep grief they are expressing in view of its discontinuance is overwhelmingly affecting to my feelings. Many of these date their subscriptions from the commencement of the paper, and they have allowed nothing in its columns to pass without a rigid scrutiny. They speak, therefore, experimentally, and "testify of that which they have seen and do know." Let them be assured that my regret in the separation which is to take place between us, in consequence of the discontinuance of the *Liberator,* is at least as poignant as their own; and let them feel, as I do, comforted by the thought that it relates only to the weekly method of communicating with each other, and not to the principles we have espoused in the past, or the hopes and aims we cherish as to the future.

Although the *Liberator* was designed to be, and has ever been, mainly devoted to the abolition of slavery, yet it has been instrumental in aiding the cause of reform in many of its most important aspects.

I have never consulted either the subscription-list of the paper or public sentiment in printing, or omitting to print, any article touching any matter whatever. Personally, I have never asked any one to become a subscriber, nor any one to contribute to its support, nor presented its claims for a better circulation in any lecture or speech, or at any one of the multitudinous anti-slavery gatherings in the land. Had I done so, no doubt its subscription-list might have been much enlarged.

In this connection, I must be permitted to express my surprise that I am gravely informed, in various quarters, that this is no time to retire from public labor; that though the chains of the captive have been broken, he is yet to be vindicated in regard to the full possession of equal civil and political rights; that the freedmen in every part of the South are subjected to many insults and outrages; that the old slave-holding spirit is showing itself in every available form; that there is imminent danger that, in the hurry of reconstruction and readmission to the Union, the late rebel States will be left free to work any amount of mischief; that there is manifestly a severe struggle yet to come with the Southern "powers of darkness," which will require the utmost vigilance and the most determined efforts on the part of the friends of impartial liberty—etc., etc., etc. Surely, it is not meant by all this that I am therefore bound to continue the publication of the *Liberator*; for that is a matter for me to determine, and no one else. As I commenced its publication without asking leave of any one, so I claim to be competent to decide when it may fitly close its career.

Again—it cannot be meant, by this presentation of the existing state of things at the South, either to impeach my intelligence, or to impute to me a lack of interest in behalf of that race for the liberation and elevation of which I have labored so many years! If, when they had no friends, and no hope of earthly redemption, I did not hesitate to make their cause my own, is it to be supposed that, with their yokes broken, and their friends and advocates multiplied indefinitely, I can be any the less disposed to stand by them to the last—to insist on the full measure of justice and equity being meted out to them—to retain in my breast a lively and permanent interest in all that relates to their present condition and future welfare?

I shall sound no trumpet and make no parade as to what I shall do for the future. After having gone through with such a struggle as has never been paralleled in duration in the life of any reformer, and for nearly forty years been the target at which all poisonous and deadly missiles have been hurled, and having seen our great national iniquity blotted out, and freedom "proclaimed throughout all the land to all the inhabitants thereof," and a thousand presses and pulpits supporting the claims of the colored population to fair treatment where not one could be found to do this in the early days of the anti-slavery conflict, I might—it seems to me—be permitted to take a little repose in my advanced years, if I desired to do so. But, as yet, I have neither asked nor wished to be relieved of any burdens or labors connected with the good old cause. I see a mighty work of enlightenment and regeneration yet to be accomplished at the South, and many cruel wrongs done to the freedmen which are yet to be redressed; and I neither counsel others to turn away from the field of conflict, under the delusion that no more remains to be done, nor contemplate such a course in my own case.

The object for which the *Liberator* was commenced—the extermination of chattel slavery—having been gloriously consummated, it seems to me specially appropriate to let its existence cover the historic period of the great struggle; leaving what remains to be done to complete the work of emancipation to other instrumentalities (of which I hope to avail myself), under new auspices, with more abundant means, and with millions instead of hundreds for allies.

Most happy am I to be no longer in conflict with the mass of my fellow-countrymen on the subject of slavery. For no man of any refinement or sensibility can be indifferent to the approbation of his fellow-men, if it be rightly earned. But to obtain it by going with the multitude to do evil—by pandering to despotic power or a corrupt public sentiment—is self-degradation and personal dishonor:

> "For more true joy Marcellus exiled feels
> Than Cæsar with a Senate at his heels."

Better to be always in a minority of one with God—branded as madman, incendiary, fanatic, heretic, infidel—frowned upon by "the
powers that be," and mobbed by the populace—or consigned igno-
miniously to the gallows, like him whose "soul is marching on," though
his "body lies mouldering in the grave," or burnt to ashes at the stake
like Wickliffe, or nailed to the cross like him who "gave himself for
the world,"—in defence of the RIGHT, than like Herod, having the
shouts of a multitude crying, "It is the voice of a god, and not of a
man!"

Farewell, tried and faithful patrons! Farewell, generous benefactors,
without whose voluntary but essential pecuniary contributions the
Liberator must have long since been discontinued! Farewell, noble
men and women who have wrought so long and so successfully, under
God, to break every yoke! Hail, ye ransomed millions! Hail, year of
jubilee! With a grateful heart and a fresh baptism of the soul, my last
invocations shall be:

> "Spirit of Freedom, on!—
>   Oh! pause not in thy flight
> Till every clime is won
>   To worship in thy light:
> Speed on thy glorious way,
>   And wake the sleeping lands!
> Millions are watching for the ray,
>   And lift to thee their hands.
> Still 'Onward!' be thy cry—
>   Thy banner on the blast;
> And, like a tempest, as thou rushest by,
>   Despots shall shrink aghast.
> On! till thy name is known
>   Throughout the peopled earth;
> On! till thou reign'st alone,
>   Man's heritage by birth;
> On! till from every vale, and where the mountains rise,
> The beacon lights of Liberty shall kindle to the skies!"

GARRISON VIEWED
BY HIS CONTEMPORARIES

13
White Abolitionists

This group of selections is from white abolitionists who became critical of Garrison's philosophy and methods; it constitutes a partial documentary history of the split in the antislavery movement as seen from the anti-Garrison perspective. The first two documents are early tributes to Garrison from men who later turned against him. Whittier's "To William Lloyd Garrison" (1832) also is the product of a deep personal friendship that antedated Garrison's career as an abolitionist. Lewis Tappan's praise of Garrison in 1833 is significant because it comes from a wealthy businessman and philanthropist who, along with his brother Arthur, was behind many of the reform movements and benevolent enterprises of the age. The Tappans were instrumental in forming the American Anti-Slavery Society.

Next comes a group of letters, by moderate abolitionists, on Garrison's 1837 controversy with the clergy of New England. For several years, Garrison had been attacking the clergy for not espousing the cause of immediate emancipation. But after 1835, his criticisms had increased in intensity, and the Congregationalists had responded by denying their pulpits to abolitionist spokesmen. Garrison then further deepened the conflict by promulgating anti-Sabbatarian views. This in turn called forth a Pastoral Letter *and two* Clerical Appeals *attacking Garrison as an enemy of Christianity, which were circulated in the Congregational churches of New England. Since many of the abolitionists believed that the antislavery cause should foster close ties with the churches, a substantial element in the movement now turned against Garrison.*

By 1839, the split within the abolitionist ranks had been

enlarged by the controversy over Garrison's espousal of Women's Rights, nonresistance, and nonparticipation in politics. To convey the anti-Garrisonians' views on the final stage of the internal struggle, I have included an account of the fight for control of the Massachusetts Anti-Slavery Society in 1839, Whittier's explanation of his break with Garrison, and two comments of Lewis Tappan's on the general situation that led to the split in the American Anti-Slavery Society in 1840.

JOHN GREENLEAF WHITTIER (1832): "TO WILLIAM LLOYD GARRISON" [1]

Champion of those who groan beneath
   Oppression's iron hand:
In view of penury, hate, and death,
   I see thee fearless stand.
Still bearing up thy lofty brow,
   In the steadfast strength of truth,
In manhood sealing well the vow
   And promise of thy youth.

Go on, for thou hast chosen well;
   On in the strength of God!
Long as one human heart shall swell
   Beneath the tyrant's rod.
Speak in a slumbering nation's ear,
   As thou hast ever spoken,
Until the dead in sin shall hear,
   The fetter's link be broken!

I love thee with a brother's love,
   I feel my pulses thrill,
To mark thy spirit soar above
   The cloud of human ill.
My heart hath leaped to answer thine,
   And echo back thy words,
As leaps the warrior's at the shine
   And flash of kindred swords!

[1] From John Greenleaf Whittier, *Poetical Works* (Boston and New York, 1892), III, 9–10.

They tell me thou art rash and vain,
  A searcher after fame;
That thou art striving but to gain
  A long-enduring name;
That thou hast nerved the Afric's hand
  And steeled the Afric's heart,
To shake aloft his vengeful brand,
  And rend his chain apart.

Have I not known thee well, and read
  Thy mighty purpose long?
And watched the trials which have made
  Thy human spirit strong?
And shall the slanderer's demon breath
  Avail with one like me,
To dim the sunshine of my faith
  And earnest trust in thee?

Go on, the dagger's point may glare
  Amid thy pathway's gloom;
The fate which sternly threatens there
  Is glorious martyrdom!
Then onward with a martyr's zeal;
  And wait thy sure reward
When man to man no more shall kneel,
  And God alone be Lord!

LEWIS TAPPAN PRAISES GARRISON (1833) [2]

Some men, Mr. President, are frightened at a name. There is good evidence to believe that many professed friends of abolition would have been here, had they not been *afraid* that the name of WILLIAM LLOYD GARRISON would be inserted prominently in our proceedings. Sir, I am ashamed of such friends. We ought to place that honored name in the forefront of our ranks. The cause is under obligations to him, which such an evidence of respect will but poorly repay.

The first time I ever heard of him was when he was in jail in Baltimore, where he was incarcerated like a felon, for pleading the cause of the oppressed, and rebuking iniquity. When I saw him, appearing so mild and meek as he does, shortly after he was liberated

[2] From a speech of Lewis Tappan at the founding convention of the American Anti-Slavery Society as reported in the *Abolitionist*, I (December, 1833).

by a gentleman in New-York, I was astonished. Is this the renegade Garrison? thought I, as I grasped his open hand. Is this the enemy of our country? I shall never forget the impression which his noble countenance made on me at that time, as long as I live.

An anecdote is related of a gentleman—a Colonizationist—which is worth repeating in this Convention. That gentleman had purchased, without knowing who it represented, a portrait of Mr. Garrison, and after having it encased in a splendid gilt frame, suspended it in his parlor. A friend calling in observed it, and asked the purchaser if he knew who he had honored so much? He was answered "No—but it is one of the most godlike looking countenances I ever beheld." "That, sir," resumed the visitor, "is a portrait of the fanatic, the incendiary William Lloyd Garrison!" "Indeed!" concluded the gentleman, evidently much disconcerted. "But, sir, it shall remain in its place. I will never take it down."

Who that is familiar with the history of Mr. Garrison does not remember the determination expressed in the first number of his paper—the *Liberator*—to sustain it *as long as could live on bread and water*? And, sir, I am informed that he has really practised what he so nobly resolved on the beginning.

Look at his course during his recent mission to England. He has been accused of slandering his country. Sir, he has vindicated the American name. He has *not* slandered it. He has told the whole truth, and put hypocrites and dough faces to open shame. He has won the confidence of the people of England. They saw him attached to his country by the dearest ties; but loathing her follies and abhorring her crimes. He has put the Anti-Slavery movement forward a quarter of a century.

A fellow passenger with Mr. Garrison from Europe—a clergyman of much intelligence—on arriving in this country heard that he was called a fanatic and a madman. "What," said he, "do you call such a man a fanatic? Do you deem such a man insane? For six weeks have I been with him, and a more discreet, humble and faithful christian I never saw."

Sir, we should throw the shield of our protection and esteem around Mr. Garrison. His life is exposed at this moment. At the door of this saloon, a young man from the South said to-day that if he had opportunity, he would dip his hands in his heart's blood. And, sir, there must be martyrs in this cause. We ought to feel this moment that we are liable to be sacrificed. But when I say this, I know that we are not belligerants. We would die in such a cause, only as martyrs to the truth. In this, our blessed Saviour has set the example.

I did not contemplate delivering a eulogy on Mr. Garrison, when I rose to speak to this resolution. I wish simply to express my heartfelt sympathy with an injured and persecuted man. Be it the honorable object of the members of this Convention to show to our countrymen that they have misunderstood the character, and misconceived the plans, of William Lloyd Garrison. He is said to be imprudent. What is prudence? Is it succumbing to a majority of our frail fellow mortals? Is it holding back a faithful expression of the whole truth, until the people are ready to say *amen?* Was that the prudence of the Apostle Paul, when he stood before the Roman Governor? Was that the prudence of William Penn, when he poured contempt on the regalia of Kings, by wearing before the king of England his broad beaver? Imprudence is moral timidity. That man is imprudent who is afraid to speak as God commands him to speak, when the hour of danger is near. If this reasoning be correct, Mr. Garrison is one of the most *prudent* men in the nation!

He is not perfect. He is frail, like the rest of human flesh. But if God had not endowed him as He has, and smiled propitiously on his imprudencies, we should not now be engaged in the deliberation of this most interesting and important Convention. God has raised up just such a man as William Lloyd Garrison, to be a pioneer in this cause. Let each member present feel solemnly bound to vindicate the character of Mr. Garrison. Let us not be afraid to go forward with him even into the "imminent breach," although there may be professed friends who stand back because of him.

HENRY B. STANTON, JAMES G. BIRNEY, AND GAMALIEL BAILEY ON GARRISON'S CONTROVERSY WITH THE CLERGY (1837) [3]

In this first letter, dated September 1, 1837, Henry B. Stanton, an abolitionist who was aligned with the New York-Ohio antislavery axis, reported events in New England to James G. Birney, one of the leaders of Western abolitionism. Prominently mentioned in this letter are Charles Fitch, Joseph H. Towne,

[3] From Dwight L. Dumond, ed., *The Letters of James Gillespie Birney* (New York, 1938), I, 420–23, 425, 428.

*James Trask Woodbury, and William Smyth, who were all lead-
ing clerical opponents of Garrison, and such supporters of Garrison as Oliver Johnson, Amos Phelps, Henry Clarke Wright,
and Ellis Gray Loring.*

. . . You probably have read the "Appeal" of Messrs. Fitch,
Towne, and others—the "Appeal" of the Andover Students, the letter
of Mr. Woodbury, the strictures of Prof. Smyth of Maine, and the
comments of the Vermont Chronicle and kindred prints, *on the one
Hand,* and the Replies of Messrs. Johnson, Garrison, and Phelps, *on
the other.* You have also seen the writings of bro. H. C. Wright, and
the use that is made of them in certain prints, to prejudice our cause.
By the N. E. Spectator, just rec'd, I see that Messrs. Fitch and Towne,
won out in reply to Garrison and Phelps, in an article of nearly 4 columns, which is to be continued next week! and tomorrow I expect to
see the Liberator containing 3 or 4 columns castigating bro. Woodbury, and the Andover Students,—and next week, in the Liberator, I
expect to see 4 or 5 columns—in reply to the "Protest" of bros. Fitch
and Towne, and then in due time, another reply to their next "Protest", and then their rejoinder, and his surrejoinder with their rebut-
ter, and his surrebutter, with occasional blows from bro. Phelps, Woodbury, Sanford etc. etc., in which much bad feeling will be mingled to
the great glee of Slaveholders and their apologists, the deep wounding
of the already bleeding cause of the Slave,—and perhaps resulting in
the organization of a new Anti Slavery Association with a new organ,
—unless the Mass. Society will cast off bro. Garrison and the Liberator.
While in and around Boston, I stood as much aloof from the whole
controversy as possible, and yet, took much pains to ascertain the true
state of the case, and how extensive was the defection (if *defection* it
may be called), and I am persuaded that the mass of the "clerical"
Abolitionists of N. England, sympathize with the sentiments advanced
by Messrs. Fitch, etc., (especially the "orthodox") and that even many
of the laity also assume the same ground. "The ice having been broken," these men are determined to push thro[ugh]; and, I am inclined
to the opinion, that, unless there is a healing balm applied to the
wound, the sore will fester beyond the power of restoration *without
amputation.* Messrs. Fitch and co-adjustors have had circulars out for
a long time, obtaining names to call a convention of "Evangelical Abo-

litionists" to organize an Evangelical Anti S. Association, *not* auxiliary
to the Am. A. S. S., but recognizing the same principles. The Spectator
was spoken of as the organ of this association. After the "Appeal" was
issued, Messrs. F. etc. received numerous letters from all parts of New
England, urging them to go forward, and approving of the Appeal.
Prominent among those from whom they rec'd these, was bro. *Woodbury*. He, as you may infer from his letter, is for pushing matters to the
extreme. He expresses himself in his speeches and in conversation, much
stronger than in his letters. Messrs. Harding, Wilder, Phelps of Groton,
Dimick, Grosvenor of Uxbridge, Wilde, Parker of Cambridgeport, etc.
etc. etc. etc. etc. take the same ground with bro. Woodbury. Of course,
the—, the Recorder, the Mirror, the Chronicle, the Andover interest,
and the Boston influence, are doing all they can to fan the flame of
contention. Woodbury etc. are open in their opposition to things as
they are, and say "they will not stand it any longer." They can sway
half the Abolitionists of New England. On the other hand, there is Garrison and his party (you know who) are resolutely bent on "war to the
knife and knife to the hilt." They will not yield an inch, to prevent the
formation of a thousand new organizations. Then there is Phelps, who
leads the ultra-radical evangelicals such as Dr. Farnsworth, Rev. Mr.
Root etc. sympathizes with Garrison, and will "go ahead." Then, there
is the *Conservative ultra party,* composed of such men as Rev. G. B.
Perry, Rev. George Allen, Ellis Gray Loring, Esq. who approve of many
things in the Appeal, but who go with all their might against a new
organization. Those are the grand divisions of our N. England Anti
Slavery army. An invincible host when contending vs. a common foe—
but powerless, and an easy prey, when contending against one another.
As things now appear, and from conversations with Phelps, Garrison,
Loring, Johnson, Perry, Farnsworth, and from what I learn direct from
Fitch, Woodbury etc. etc. etc. etc. there is to be a very unpleasant warfare carried on (I fear a war of extermination between two of the parties) and which will destroy, or at all events, greatly cripple our cause
in N. England, unless there is an *umpire influence* exerted *here,* which
shall settle the dispute, and attach all parties to the American A. S.
Soc., with such small losses as would be benificial [*sic*] rather than
detrimental. Such an influence *can be,* and I trust *will be* exerted here
by our Ex. Com.—danger is, we shall loose [*sic*] either the Fitch or
Woodbury party, or the Garrison and part of the Phelps party. *We
need them all.* Our cause can never succeed in N. E. unless we can

attach to it the former party,— Never! Garrison (*inter nos*) would not yield the tithe of a hair in *peculiarity of expression* nor in *principle,* to save them all! Besides,—things were shaping into an attitude to bring over the mass of moral influence in N. England fully to our side, (the Edwardses, the Lords, the Channings) when lo! this Explosion; And even *now* if the lava is wisely conducted off the commotion will subside, and they will yet be with us. WHO IS TO DO THE WORK? Under God, I believe we must look to the Ex. Com. of the Am. Soc. to steer the ship thro[ugh]. . . .

> *James G. Birney gave a clear indication of his own response to "the Boston controversy" in a letter of September 14, 1837, to Lewis Tappan. "I greatly lament the course Mr. Garrison seems to be taking," he wrote, "I have been disappointed in him. . . . I have no expectation that G. can be reduced to moderation, and I am not prepared to say, that his departure from us may not be the best thing he could do for the cause of Emancipation." Another moderate abolitionist, Gamaliel Bailey of New York expressed similar sentiments in a less reserved manner in discussing Garrison's attack on the clergy in a letter to Birney on October 14, 1837.*

As to the Boston controversy—my heart is sick. I try to restrain myself, but the disgusting gross egotism of Garrison, and the loathsome adulation of his idolators, are continually urging me to say something in the *Philanthropist.* Have you read his letter to J. T. Woodbury? He compares himself to an Apostle—he has called out such men as A. Tappan, J. G. Birney, Gerrit Smith etc. etc. He is the Atlas of abolition. Had not God made *his* forehead strong against the foreheads of the people, the bark of abolition would have been wrecked on the rocks and quicksands of human expediency. So he says. I believe in my soul, we have all overvalued Garrison. And as to himself, pride has driven him mad. I cannot bear to see this ignoble idolatry among abolitionists. To use a word of Dr. Channing, I reverence human nature too much, to look without pain, on that man, who will prostrate himself before anything but the power of Truth and the throne of God. Whatever may be my feelings, however, I will always try to consult the good of the cause.

STANTON, WHITTIER, AND LEWIS TAPPAN
ON THE SCHISMS OF 1839–40

Henry B. Stanton, acting once again as a source of intelligence for the New York-Ohio abolitionists, provided the following description of the 1839 meeting of the Massachusetts Anti-Slavery Society in a letter to Birney, dated January 26, 1839.

. . . our meeting. . . . was stormy enough. But, it has developed the disease in the Anti-Slavery body, which has been too long concealed under the surface. Garrison found himself pushed to the wall on the non-government question, and with his train bands, he made a desperate push to sway the Society over to his non-resistance views. He succeeded. A resolution, declaring it to be the duty of such abolitionists as can conscientiously exercise the elective franchise, to go to the polls and vote for the slave, was strenuously oppossed [sic] by him and voted down. Fowler, of Westfield, O. Scott, St. Clair, Wise, Phelps, Geo. Allen, and all that stamp of men, were browbeaten down. In fact, they were well nigh mobbed down by the non-resistants. Whenever one of those men rose to speak, men would cry out, "no matter what they say—no matter what they propose—let us vote them down!" When I was about to speak on the subject of a new paper, and had the floor, it was yielded by me that a paper might be read to the meeting, and behold, that paper was a motion to restrict the speakers to 15 minutes! The gag was thus, by deception, thrust into my mouth. I took it very calmly. The next day, in the course of my remarks, I asserted that Garrison said in 1834, that he should cast his vote not for Abbot[t] Lawrence for Congress, but for Amasa Walker (we were trying to find out what the term "political action" meant, as used in our early documents) Garrison shouted out "it is false" "it is false," and challenged the proof. Oliver Johnson re-echoed the shout. Afterwards, when I came forward with a file of the Liberator and offered to read the proof, I was denied the privelege [sic]. But, I cared nothing for this, and only mention it as an illustration of the unfairness with which the whole proceedings were conducted. But, the point is,—the Society hauled down its flag and run up the crazy banner of the non-government heresy, and we had to rally around or be ostracised. The split is wide, and can never be closed up. Mr. Fowler looked on very calmly, and told me that it was utterly in vain for us to undertake to work together. A very large corps of Methodists were present, and went right and with their whole hearts, almost to a man. Scott told me that the Methodists generally in the State would go against all these distracting *isms*. Our cause in this State is ruined unless we can seperate [*sic*] the A. S. Society from everything which does not belong to it. That is the issue now tendered to us, and meet it we must, sooner or later. I am for meeting it here, now, on the spot where the evil exists. Don't be alarmed about Mass. Abolitionism. It is sound. The *pledged* delegates from Lynn and Boston carried through the report and voted down political action. But Lynn and Boston are not all the Commonwealth. If they were, the whole abolition fabric in the State would be in ruins, and we should be compelled to erect a new Society out of the fragments. Nil desperandum etc.

We have resolved upon a new paper. This is our grand move. It will purge us from the poison in 12 or 15 months. 2200 subscribers are pledged. We have got a Committee and are going ahead. We want an Editor. We have set our eyes upon bro. E. Wright Jr.

I shall be in N. Y. next Tuesday, and will talk the whole matter over with you. But, I wish our friends distinctly to understand, that Garrisonism and Abolitionism in this State, are contending for the mastery. Love to God and love to the slave *impell* me to stand and battle for the Right and the True.

I have just got hold of the resolution above mentioned, which the Society voted down:—"Resolved, that it is the imperious duty of every abolitionist, who can conscientiously exercise the elective franchise, to go promptly to the polls and deposite [*sic*] his vote in favor of some man, who, if elected, will use his utmost Constitutional power for the immediate overthrow of slavery.". . .[4]

John Greenleaf Whittier, previously one of Garrison's most faithful followers, broke with him in 1839 over the question of the relation of nonresistance to the antislavery cause. Whittier's side of the argument was presented in the Pennsylvania Freeman *and reprinted in the* Liberator *of July 12, 1839. After quoting Garrison to the effect that abolitionist espousal of nonresistance will aid the cause of emancipation, Whittier goes on as follows:*

[4] From Dwight L. Dumond, ed., *The Letters of James Gillespie Birney* (New York, 1938), I, 481–83.

Now in all this we doubt not our brother Garrison is entirely sincere. With one of his intellectual temperament, to *believe* is to *know;* doubt is inadmissible. He believes in the sincerity of his heart that his new religious doctrines are *"destined to pour new life blood into the veins of abolition, and preserve it from corruption,"* hence, *as an abolitionist* even, he feels bound to advocate them in his paper, as he has done for the last three years.

Now, *we* may believe that the doctrines of the Society of Friends, if generally adopted by abolitionists, would be beneficial even to their abolitionism. What then? Shall we make the Freeman a *sectarian* paper; and divide our attention so nearly between assaults upon slavery and animadversions upon creeds, ceremonials, and a hired ministry, as to make it difficult to decide for what purpose it was established?

We readily admit, that strictly speaking, the Liberator is not the official organ of any abolition society. But it is held forth to the world as *"the organ of the great anti-slavery movement."* Hence by a stronger reason should that paper of all others, as the recognized organ of THE CAUSE itself, be held entirely aloof from the sectarian views of its editor. Let it present nothing but pure unadulterated abolitionism. Let that stand forth in its distinct and perfect beauty. Let its editor, *as its editor,* be known only as the friend of the suffering and dumb. Let his fervid zeal—his solemn and impressive language—his "words of weight and fire" have their full effect upon the mind and heart of the reader, divested of any extraneous prejudice and totally disconnected with the sectarian sentiments above alluded to. In a word, let the slave have the Liberator as his own. Let its banner, as it unrolls to the eye of the task-masters of America, bear no other inscription than that of "ABOLITION." Let it be, as at the beginning, a sign of hope and promise to the bondman: a warning and rebuke to the oppressor. Whatever its editor may feel himself called upon to do in another capacity—whatever sentiments he may embrace on other topics, we conjure him, in the name of all that's precious in our cause —in the name of the very peace which he advocates—in the name of the millions of our enslaved countrymen, and of their dreadful reality of suffering,—to make the Liberator indeed and *ONLY,* "the organ of the *Anti-Slavery* movement." [5]

In his journal for June 6, 1839, Lewis Tappan commented on the decision of the anti-Garrisonians in Massachusetts to form

[5] From the *Liberator* (Boston), July 12, 1839.

a new antislavery society as a response to their defeat at the January convention.

I rejoice that a new society is formed in Massachusetts. Garrison and others have grown lukewarm on the anti-slavery subject and have loaded the cause with their no-government—woman's rights—non-resistant etc. notions until we have got among [the] breakers. Garrison told me 2½ years ago that these were subjects he considered paramount to the anti-slavery cause, to which he meant to devote his attention chiefly. It is a sad mistake, I think in him to vault from the anti-slavery cause or to attempt to make it instrumental in carrying out other matters.[6]

The following year the schism in Massachusetts was reproduced on the national level, when Garrison seized control of the American Anti-Slavery Society, forcing the withdrawal of a large group which then formed a new organization—the American and Foreign Anti-Slavery Society. The immediate cause of the split was a vote on the question of whether or not women should serve on the Society's committees. Tappan gave his interpretation of this event in a letter to Theodore Weld dated May 26, 1840.

Brother Weld,
I want you to consider the following things—
1. The *split* was not *solely* on account of the claim that women shall vote, speak, be on committees, be officers, etc.
2. It was not [at] all because [of] opposition to their being *members* of the Society.
3. But it was chiefly because Garrison and his party (for although he and a few others profess *not* to speak the sentiments of the major part of the old M[assachusett]s Soc. yet it is evident they follow W. L. G's beck in everything) foisted upon the Amer. Anti Soc. the woman question, no government question, etc., and the bad spirit shown by the Liberator, etc.
4. When the Constitution of the A. Anti S. Soc. was formed in 1833,

[6] From the Tappan Papers, Library of Congress.

and the word "person" introduced, *all concerned* considered that it was to be understood as it is usually understood in our benevolent Societies. All have a right to be *members,* but the *business* to be conducted by the men. This understanding continued for 6 years. W. L. G. so understood it. See Phelps's remark in M's. Abolitionist.

5. W. L. G. introduced the question into the Anti S. Soc. to make an experiment upon the public. He had avowed before that there were subjects paramount to the Anti S. cause. And he was using the Society as an instrument to establish these notions. Since he introduced this question the slave has been lost sight of mainly. I add no more. See the Reporter.

L. T.

Women have equal rights with men, and therefore they have a right to form societies of women only. Men have the same right. *Men* formed the Amer. Anti S. Society.[7]

[7] From Gilbert H. Barnes and Dwight L. Dumond, ed., *Grimke Letters of Theodore Dwight Weld, Angelina Weld, and Sarah Grimke, 1822–1844* (New York, 1934), II, 836. Reprinted by permission of Elizabeth Barnes Pumphrey and Dwight L. Dumond.

14

Negro Abolitionists

Most of the original subscribers to the Liberator *were Northern free Negroes, and Garrison maintained a devoted Negro following throughout his career. The following descriptions of Garrison are by Negro leaders and reveal his pre-eminence, in their minds, among white abolitionists. They show also that Negro abolitionists could disagree with Garrison and reject his advice. As far as the Negro community was concerned, Garrison was a useful ally but not an infallible leader.*

THEODORE S. WRIGHT: A TRIBUTE TO GARRISON FROM A NEGRO MINISTER [1]

Immediately after the insurrection in Virginia, under Nat Turner, we saw colonization spreading all over the land; and it was popular to say the people of color must be removed. . . . Benj. Lundy, of Baltimore nobly lifted up his voice. But he did not feel the vileness of colonization. A young man, for making certain expositions touching slavery was incarcerated in a dungeon, where truth took a lodgment in his heart, where he avowed eternal hatred to slavery, and where, before high heaven, in the secrecy of his dungeon, with the chains upon him, he resolved to devote his life to the cause of emancipation. And when the president of the American Anti-Slavery Society stepped forward and paid the fine, we were crying for help, we were remonstrating.— We had no other means but to stand up as men, and protest. We declared, this is our country, and our home;—here are the graves of our fathers. But none came to the rescue. At that dark moment we heard a voice; it was the voice of Garrison, speaking in trumpet tones. It was like the voice of an angel of mercy. Hope, hope then

<hr>

[1] From a speech by the Rev. Theodore S. Wright at the meeting of the New York State Anti-Slavery Society, 1837, reprinted in the *Liberator* (Boston), October 13, 1837.

cheered our path. The signs of the times began to indicate brighter days.

CHARLES B. RAY: NEGRO ABOLITIONISTS
AND THE SCHISM OF 1840 [2]

This letter from Charles B. Ray, a leading Negro editor, to Henry B. Stanton and James G. Birney, suggests the problems created for Negro abolitionists by the 1840 split in the antislavery movement. Garrison, about to leave for the World Anti-Slavery convention, sought exclusive endorsement for his delegation from a meeting of New York Negroes—an action that could signify Negro repudiation of a rival delegation from the anti-Garrison or "New Organization" group. Among those in attendence, in addition to Ray, were such prominent Negro abolitionists as Thomas Van Rensalaer and the Rev. Henry Highland Garnett.

On the 17th ultimo, Bro. T. Van Rensalaer between meetings, (it being Sunday) suggested to me the propriety as he thought, of having a meeting of the colored people, to hear an address from our old and tried FRIEND MR. GARRISON, and as he was to leave us the day following for LONDON to attend the worlds convention, to pass some resolutions expressive of our confidence in him, as a delegate, to said convention. I objected to aid him in getting up a meeting for that object alone, on the grounds as I stated to him, that other men had gone, who were dear to us as a *colored community,* and if we were going to express our confidence in one as a delegate, we should do the same to all, and not make such an invidious distinction, which in my opinion was unjust. The Rev. Tho L. Wright, concur[r]ed with my views. Mr. Van Rensalaer deemed them satisfactory and judicious, as we thought, whereupon the House was granted, and I exerted myself to notify the meeting. Three of us, Mr. Van Rensalaer being one, resolved ourselves into a committee, to draft resolutions for the meeting, and were to meet at my office at 4 o'clock. Upon presenting our resolutions in committee, Mr. Van Rensalaer presented but one and that expressive of our views of the Convention to be held, and our confidence in four only, of the delegation, those who were taken up by the

[2] From a letter of Charles B. Ray to Stanton and Birney, May 20, 1840, in *Birney Letters,* ed. Dwight L. Dumond, I, 576–78.

AMERICAN SOCIETY, upon the third day of the meeting. We objected to the resolution as perverting the meeting from its avowed object and contrary to the notices given, and a violation of the conditions upon which the House was obtained, and I had consented to cooperate in getting up the meeting, and because it was a negative disapproval of all the other delegates to be present from this country, who were alike entitled to our approbation and love, and as the resolution if passed, would be presented to the convention, it would place those other delegates in awkward position, and be both unfair and unjust. Mr. Van Rensalaer, determined to accept no amendment, we waived the matter untill [sic] it should be presented to the meeting, informing him, that then, it should be amended if passed, or else it should be laid aside.

The meeting convened in the Rev. Mr. WRIGHTS CHURCH, a very respectable audience both as to number and character. The Rev. Bro. Wright in the chair, and myself appointed Secretary.

After an address of some length, from our FRIEND MR. GARRISON, MR. VAN RENSALAER, immediately arose and presented his resolution. Bro. H. H. Garnett, of Oneida Institute, seconded the resolution and moved an amendment to insert your names as delegates also virtually appointed, by the AMERICAN SOCIETY. This not meeting my objections, Mr. J. J. Tuille, a clercke [sic] in our Office, moved an amendment to Mr. Garnetts amendment, and I suggested an improvement to his, so that it should read "we approve of the American delegation, sent out by American Abolitionists" for we knew them all, either personally or by reputation. The whole matter elicited some considerable debate, all excepting Mr. Van Rensalaer, in favour of the amendments. Some however thought we had better take no action upon the matter, and after hearing some remarks from MR. GARRISON in which he objected to have his name associated with yours, and Mr. Colver's, remarks which the meeting were very sorry to hear, and which they were not prepared to receive, and it now being late, I moved the indefinite postponement of the whole subject, which was carried.

We could easily have passed a resolution, approving of the entire delegation, had it not been so late, but any other invidious resolution, could not have been passed by that meeting, not because we were wanting in respect for any, but because we had too much real regard for all.

Now this refusal to pass an *illiberal* resolution (taken in its relation to the delegation) expressing our confidence in and approval of a few of the delegation of which Bro. Garrison was one, to the rejection of the many, Bro. Rogers regards as an alienation of feeling, and respect towards Mr. Garrison and this alienation of affection, as he regards it, Bro. Rogers is going to show as he says and as I am informed by Bro. Van Rensalaer as one of the fruits of New Organization as tho[ugh] nothing else could effect our minds toward MR. GARRISON if affected at all, but New Organization, a conclusion more unfounded and more unfair, in relation to us, could hardly have been arrived at.

If the colored people of this City, or any section of this country, do manifest less warmth of feeling, than formerly towards *Mr. Garrison* it is in part oweing [*sic*] to our *Friends* haveing [*sic*] multiplied who are equally active, and equally efficient with *Mr. Garrison,* and as a necessary consequence our good feeling is scattered upon all, instead of being concentrated upon one, as when Mr. Garrison stood alone. But there is another reason, and which I intended to have mentioned to Mr. Garrison personally, but had not the time when I saw him, viz the spirit with which Bro. Garrison has conducted his own PAPER since this controversy commenced, especially the repeated use which he made of Bro. Wrights letter to yourself.

These things affected some of our intelligent brethren, as they have informed me, and not *New Organization,* however much that may have a tendency to alienate feeling from Bro. Garrison. I give you this history of the meeting by no means in defence of New Organization, but that you may have the facts to prevent any wronge [*sic*] impression that might be made, by B. Rogers from his want of a knowledge of the true state of the case, and that it might not appear in England that we have forsaken our friends, but are constrained to cleave to all. We look forward to the worlds convention with great interest. We anticipate the happiest results from its proceedings, especially if you do not drag in foreign matters which may God prevent. We are proud in a proper sense, of our American delegation, and no man is an exception. We know you as men having passed through the ordeal that tried mens souls, and now hardly having escaped, you are not going to form an alliance with the enemy. We regret that some more of us cannot be with you. We hope, we pray that the enslaved of the world, those held in a chattle [*sic*] sense, of all colors and of all climes, may be the object of your deliberations, and that the result of them may be to raise up mankind to all the dignity of free men. We hope our American delegation, will meet together in London and altho[ugh] they have differed here, that they will bury the hatchet, and do nothing to reflect upon our holy cause in this our beloved tho[ugh] slavery ridden country.

FREDERICK DOUGLASS ON GARRISON [3]

The most celebrated of all Negro abolitionists was Frederick Douglass, the escaped slave who became a powerful antislavery orator. Until the 1850's, Douglass worked closely with Garrison and subscribed in general to his philosophy of abolition. The first two selections included below, both from 1847, are eloquent tributes to Garrison. The first is from Douglass's farewell address to the British people, and the second is from a letter of August 20 to Sidney Howard Gay describing a speaking tour in Ohio that Douglass and Garrison were making together. The last excerpt is from a lecture of 1855. By this time, Douglass had broken with Garrison, and this lecture contains his mature assessment of the Garrisonian movement.

Sir, the foremost, strongest, and mightiest among those who have completely identified themselves with the Negroes in the United States, I will now name here; and I do so because his name has been most unjustly coupled with odium in this country. [Hear, hear.] I will name, if only as an expression of gratitude on my part, my beloved, esteemed, and almost venerated friend, William Lloyd Garrison. [Loud and prolonged cheering.] Sir, I have now been in this country for nineteen months; I have gone through its length and breadth; I have had sympathy here and sympathy there; co-operation here, and co-operation there; in fact, I have scarcely met a man who has withheld friendship from me as an abolitionist, standing unconnected with William Lloyd Garrison. [Hear.] Had I stood disconnected from that great and good man, then numerous and influential parties would have held out to me the right hand of fellowship, sanctioned my proceedings in England, backed me up with money and praise, and have given me a great reputation, so far as they were capable; and they were men of influence. And why, sir, is William Lloyd Garrison hated and despised by certain parties in this country? What has he done to deserve such treatment

[3] From Philip S. Foner, *The Life and Writings of Frederick Douglass* (New York, 1950), I, 217–18, 259–60; II, 350–52. Copyright © 1950 by International Publishers Co., Inc. Reprinted by permission of International Publishers Co., Inc.

at their hands? He has done that which all great reformers and pioneers in the cause of freedom or religion have ever been called upon to do— made himself unpopular for life in the maintenance of great principles. He has thrown himself, as it were, over the ditch as a bridge; his own body, his personal reputation, his individual property, his wide and giant-hearted intellect, all were sacrificed to form a bridge that others might pass over and enjoy a rich reward from the labours that he had bestowed, and the seed which he had sown. He has made himself disreputable. How? By his uncompromising hostility to slavery, by his bold, scathing denunciation of tyranny; his unwavering inflexible adherence to principle; and by his frank, open, determined spirit of opposition to everything like cant and hypocrisy. [Loud cheers.] Such is the position in which he stands among the American people. And the same feeling exists in this country to a great extent. Because William Lloyd Garrison has upon both sides of the Atlantic fearlessly unmasked hypocrisy, and branded impiety in language in which impiety deserves to be characterized, he has thereby brought down upon himself the fierce execrations of a religious party in this land.

*   *   *

. . . Mr. Garrison is the honoured centre of every circle into whose midst we are brought. His conversational powers are inexhaustible; he seems as fresh at midnight as at midday. Our friends eagerly flock around to hear his words of strength and cheer, while our enemies as eagerly draw around to catch him in his words. The former go away delighted with the man, while the latter skulk away, disappointed and chagrined, that they have found so little at which to be offended. Mr. Garrison's visit must do much to disabuse the public mind in this region, and to produce a mighty reaction in favour of radical Eastern Abolitionism. The Liberty party, and pro-slavery papers, have overshot themselves in regard to him.— They have so maligned and slandered him, and have so distorted, perverted, and misrepresented his views, that they have created the most intense curiosity among the people to see and hear him, and having associated his person with the representations of his mind, that his bare presence, without the utterance of a word, is all sufficient to create an impression most favourable to him, and at once to dispel the dread, and gloomy apprehensions created concerning him. When he opens his mouth, and pours forth his truthful voice, the dark and foul spirit of slander falls before him, like Dagon before the ark. People come expecting to see a fierce, proud, ambitious, and bitter looking man, a gloomy spirit, altogether dissatisfied with himself, and all the world around him; a stranger to peace, a man of war, if not of blood; completely wrapped up within the narrow limits of a single idea, perfectly above everything interesting to other men, an infidel, atheist, and madman, rejoicing over the triumphs of evil, and inflexibly bent upon the destruction of everything good. Such is the man which the pious, and pro-slavery papers of our land have taught the honest "Buckeyes" to look for in the person of William Lloyd Garrison, and in seeing him, they readily perceive how great has been the deception practiced upon them, and very naturally many of them are filled with indignation and loathing, for their mean and dastardly deceivers. . . .

* * *

I shall consider, first, the Garrisonian Anti-Slavery Society. I call this the Garrisonian Society, because Mr. Garrison is, confessedly, its leader. This Society is the oldest of modern Anti-Slavery Societies. It has, strictly speaking, two weekly papers, or organs—employs five or six lecturers—and holds numerous public meetings for the dissemination of its views. Its peculiar and distinctive feature is, its doctrine of *"no union with slaveholders."* This doctrine has, of late, become its bond of union, and the condition of good fellowship among its members. Of this Society, I have to say, its logical result is but negatively, anti-slavery. Its doctrine, of "no union with slaveholders," carried out, dissolves the Union, and leaves the slaves and their masters to fight their own battles, in their own way. This I hold to be an abandonment of the great idea with which that Society started. It started to free the slave. It ends by leaving the slave to free himself. It started with the purpose to imbue the heart of the nation with sentiments favorable to the abolition of slavery, and ends by seeking to free the North from all responsibility of slavery, other than if slavery were in Great Britain, or under some other nationality. This, I say, is the practical abandonment of the idea, with which that Society started. It has given up the faith, that the slave can be freed short of the overthrow of the Government; and then, as I understand that Society, it leaves the slaves, as it must needs leave them, just where it leaves the slaves of Cuba, or those of Brazil. The nation, as such, is given up as beyond the power of salvation by the foolishness of preaching; and hence, the aim is now to save the North; so that the American Anti-Slavery Society, which was inaugurated to convert the nation, after ten years' struggle, parts with its faith, and aims now to save the North. One of the most eloquent of all the members of that Society, and the man who is only second to Mr. Garrison himself, defines the Garrisonian doctrine thus:

> All the slave asks of us, is to stand out of his way, withdraw our pledge to keep the peace on the plantation; withdraw our pledge to return him; withdraw that representation which the Constitution gives in proportion to the number of slaves, and without any agitation here, without any individual virtue, which the times have eaten out of us, God will vindicate the oppressed, by the laws of justice which he has founded. Trample under foot your own unjust pledges, break to pieces your compact with hell by which you become the abettors of oppression. Stand alone, and let no cement of the Union bind the slave, and he will right himself.

That is it. "Stand alone"; the slave is to "right himself." I dissent entirely from this reasoning. It assumes to be true what is plainly absurd, and that is, that a population of slaves, without arms, without means of concert, and without leisure, is more than a match for double its number, educated, accustomed to rule, and in every way prepared for warfare, offensive or defensive. This Society, therefore, consents to leave the slave's freedom to a most uncertain and improbable, if not an impossible, contingency.

But, *"no union with slaveholders."*

As a mere expression of abhorrence of slavery, the sentiment is a good one; but it expresses no intelligible principle of action, and throws no light on the pathway of duty. Defined, as its authors define it, it leads to false doctrines, and mischievous results. It condemns Gerrit Smith for sitting in Congress, and our Savior for eating with publicans and sinners. Dr. Spring uttered a shocking sentiment, when he said, if one prayer of his would emancipate every slave, he would not offer that prayer. No less shocking is the sentiment of the leader of the disunion forces, when he says, that if one vote of his would emancipate every slave in this country, he would not cast that vote. Here, on a bare theory, and for a theory which, if consistently adhered to, would drive a man out of the world—a theory which can never be made intelligible to common sense—the freedom of the whole slave population would be sacrificed.

But again: "no union with slaveholders." I dislike the morality of this sentiment, in its application to the point at issue. For instance: A. unites with B. in stealing my property, and carrying it away to California, or to Australia, and, while there, Mr. A. becomes convinced that he did wrong in stealing my property, and says to Mr. B., "no union with property stealers," and abandons him, leaving the property in his hands. Now, I put it to this audience, has Mr. A., in this trans- action, met the requirements of stringent morality? He, certainly, has not. It is not only his duty to separate from the thief, but to restore the stolen property to its rightful owner. And I hold that in the Union, this very thing of restoring to the slave his long-lost rights, can better be accomplished than it can possibly be accomplished outside of the Union. This, then, is my answer to the motto, "No union with slave- holders."

But this is not the worst fault of this Society. Its chief energies are expended in confirming the opinion, that the United States Consti- tution is, and was, intended to be a slave-holding instrument—thus piling up, between the slave and his freedom, the huge work of the abolition of the Government, as an indispensable condition to emanci- pation. My point here is, first, the Constitution is, according to its read- ing, an anti-slavery document; and, secondly, to dissolve the Union, as a means to abolish slavery, is about as wise as it would be to burn up this city, in order to get the thieves out of it. But again, we hear the motto, "no union with slaveholders"; and I answer it, as that noble champion of liberty, N. P. Rogers, answered it with a more sensible motto, namely—*"No union with slaveholding."* I would unite with anybody to do right; and with nobody to do wrong. And as the Union, under the Constitution, requires me to do nothing which is wrong, and gives me many facilities for doing good, I cannot go with the American Anti-Slavery Society in its doctrine of disunion.

15

Lyman Beecher and William Ellery Channing: Moderate Reformers

Two of the period's leading spokesmen for benevolence and moderate reform were the Rev. William Ellery Channing and the Rev. Lyman Beecher. Channing, a Unitarian, and Beecher, a Congregationalist, were bitter theological opponents, but they were alike in their reluctance to give full support to the abolitionist movement. Beecher, as President of Lane Seminary, in Cincinnati, suppressed a debate on slavery among the students in 1834, with the result that most of the students withdrew from the institution. He later provided leadership to the clerical opposition to Garrison in New England. Channing took the position of friendly critic of the abolitionists and attempted in his writings on slavery to point out the evils of "the peculiar institution," while at the same time criticizing the abolitionists for their extremism.

Beecher's opinion of Garrison and his role is set forth in his autobiography and indicates a desire to take credit for Garrison as a product of the evangelical movement while at the same time repudiating Garrison's style of reform (which he viewed as a judgment of God upon the wicked). Beecher's comment, which he wrote in the third person, is an example of the kind of equivocation that was characteristic of his pronouncements on reform issues.

The first number of the Liberator was issued January, 1831, a few months after Dr. Beecher received his call to Lane Seminary. Confessing himself to have been till September, 1829, the advocate of gradual emancipation, the editor defines his present and future position by the emphatic menace, "Let Southern oppressors tremble! Let their secret abettors tremble! Let all the enemies of the persecuted blacks tremble!"

The interval between this challenge and 1837, while gradually destroying Mr. Garrison's original sympathy with the theology of revivals and its kindred developments, added constantly to the intensity and power of his appeals. Yet the fact of this divergence of the Liberator from the theology of the Puritans does not nullify the fact that it was itself the child of that theology, albeit a wayward child. Its first numbers speak the dialect of Canaan—the dialect of faith, and prayer, and evangelical sympathy. "Take away the Bible," it exclaims (April 2, 1831), "and our warfare with oppression, and infidelity, and intemperance, and impurity, and crime is at an end; our weapons are wrested away, our foundation is removed; we have no authority to speak, and no courage to act."

Religious revivals, it says, "are scriptural occurrences; without them the promises of God would fail, and the earth be flooded with iniquity. If the kingdoms of this world are to become the kingdoms of our Lord and of his Christ, the event can never come to pass independent of great revivals."

The jargon of Ashdod was later learned, taught by impatience under tribulation, and exasperation at the sins of good men.

It was really the power of the Puritan theology, whose impetus remained long after its distinctive spirit was lost, beneath which the guilty nation was heaving and surging like the ocean before the impending tempest of divine judgment. "I regard," writes Dr. Beecher, March, 1838,

the whole abolition movement, under its most influential leaders, with its distinctive maxims and modes of feeling, and also the whole temper, principles, and action of the South in the justification of slavery, as signal instances of infatuation permitted by Heaven for purposes of national retribution. God never raised up such men as Garrison, and others like him, as the ministers of his mercy for purposes of peaceful reform, but only as the fit and fearful ministers of his vengeance upon a people incorrigibly wicked.[1]

The following discussion of abolitionism from Channing's Essay on Slavery *(1835) does not specifically mention Garrison, but the whole tenor of the argument indicates that Channing has Garrison and his followers chiefly in mind.*

[1] From Barbara M. Cross, ed., *The Autobiography of Lyman Beecher* (Cambridge, Mass., 1961), II, 320 f. Reprinted by permission of the Belknap Press of Harvard University Press.

The word ABOLITIONIST, in its true meaning, comprehends every man who feels himself bound to exert his influence for removing slavery. It is a name of honorable import, and was worn, not long ago, by such men as Franklin and Jay. Events, however, continually modify terms; and, of late, the word Abolitionist has been narrowed from its original import, and restricted to the members of associations formed among us to promote Immediate Emancipation. It is not without reluctance that I give up to a small body a name which every good man ought to bear. But to make myself intelligible, and to avoid circumlocution, I shall use the word in what is now its common acceptation.

I approach this subject unwillingly, because it will be my duty to censure those, whom at this moment I would on no account hold up to public displeasure. The persecutions, which the Abolitionists have suffered and still suffer, awaken only my grief and indignation, and incline me to defend them to the full extent which truth and justice will admit. To the persecuted of whatever name my sympathies are pledged, and especially to those who are persecuted in a cause substantially good. I would not for worlds utter a word to justify the violence recently offered to a party, composed very much of men blameless in life, and holding the doctrine of non-resistance to injuries; and of women, exemplary in their various relations, and acting, however mistakenly, from benevolent and pious impulses.

Of the Abolitionists I know very few; but I am bound to say of these, that I honor them for their strength of principle, their sympathy with their fellow-creatures, and their active goodness. As a party, they are singularly free from political and religious sectarianism, and have been distinguished by the absence of management, calculation, and worldly wisdom. That they have ever proposed or desired insurrection or violence among the slaves, there is no reason to believe. All their principles repel the supposition. It is a remarkable fact, that, though the South and the North have been leagued to crush them, though they have been watched by a million of eyes, and though prejudice has been prepared to detect the slightest sign of corrupt communication with the slave, yet this crime has not been fastened on a single member of this body. . . .

The charge of corrupt design, so vehemently brought against the Abolitionists, is groundless. The charge of fanaticism I have no desire to repel. But in the present age it will not do to deal harshly with the characters of fanatics. They form the mass of the people. Religion and Politics, Philanthropy and Temperance, Nullification and Anti-masonry, the Levelling Spirit of the working man, and the Spirit of Speculation in the man of business, all run into fanaticism. This is the type of all our epidemics. A sober man who can find? The Abolition-ists have but caught the fever of the day. That they should have escaped would have been a moral miracle.— I offer these remarks simply from a sense of justice. Had not a persecution, without parallel in our country, broken forth against this society, I should not have spoken a word in their defence. But whilst I have power, I owe it to the Persecuted. If they have laid themselves open to the laws, let them suffer. For all their errors and sins let the tribunal of public opinion inflict the full measure of rebuke which they deserve. I ask no favor for them. But they shall not be stripped of the rights of man, of rights guaranteed by the laws and Constitution, without one voice, at least, being raised in their defence.

The Abolitionists have done wrong, I believe; nor is their wrong to be winked at, because done fanatically or with good intention; for how much mischief may be wrought with good design! They have fallen into the common error of enthusiasts, that of taking too narrow views, of feeling as if no evil existed but that which they opposed, and as if no guilt could be compared with that of countenancing or upholding it. The tone of their newspapers, as far as I have seen them, has often been fierce, bitter, exasperating. Their imaginations have fed too much on pictures of the cruelty to which the slave is exposed, till not a few have probably conceived of his abode as perpetually re-sounding with the lash, and ringing with shrieks of agony. I know that many of their publications have been calm, well considered, abounding in strong reasoning, and imbued with an enlightened love of freedom. But some, which have been most widely scattered, and are most adapted to act on the common mind, have had a tone un-friendly both to manners and to the spirit of our religion. I doubt not that the majority of the Abolitionists condemn the coarseness and violence of which I complain. But in this, as in most associations, the many are represented and controlled by the few, and are made to sanc-tion and become responsible for what they disapprove.

One of their errors has been the adoption of "Immediate Emanci-pation" as their motto. To this they owe not a little of their unpopu-larity. This phrase has contributed much to spread far and wide the belief, that they wished immediately to free the slave from all his restraints. They made explanations; but thousands heard the motto who never saw the explanation; and it is certainly unwise for a party to choose a watchword, which can be rescued from misapprehension only by labored explication. It may also be doubted, whether they ever removed the objection which their language so universally raised, whether they have not always recommended a precipitate action, inconsistent with the well-being of the slave and the order of the state.

Another objection to their movements is, that they have sought to accomplish their objects by a system of Agitation; that is, by a system of affiliated societies, gathered, and held together, and extended, by passionate eloquence. This, in truth, is the common mode by which all projects are now accomplished. The age of individual action is gone. Truth can hardly be heard unless shouted by a crowd. The weightiest argument for a doctrine is the number which adopts it. Accordingly, to gather and organize multitudes is the first care of him who would remove an abuse or spread a reform. That the expedient is in some cases useful, is not denied. But generally it is a showy, noisy mode of action, appealing to the passions, and driving men into exaggeration; and there are special reasons why such a mode should not be employed in regard to slavery; for slavery is so to be opposed as not to exasperate the slave, or endanger the community in which he lives. The Abolitionists might have formed an association; but it should have been an elective one. Men of strong moral principle, judiciousness, sobriety, should have been carefully sought as members. Much good might have been accomplished by the coöperation of such philanthropists. Instead of this, the Abolitionists sent forth their orators, some of them transported with fiery zeal, to sound the alarm against slavery through the land, to gather together young and old, pupils from schools, females hardly arrived at years of discretion, the ignorant, the excitable, the impetuous, and to organize these into associations for the battle against oppression. They preached their doctrine to the colored people, and collected these into their societies. To this mixed and excitable multitude, appeals were made in the piercing tones of passion; and slaveholders were held up as monsters of cruelty and crime. Now to this procedure I must object, as unwise, as unfriendly to the spirit of Christianity, and as increasing, in a degree, the perils of the Slaveholding States. Among the unenlightened, whom they so powerfully addressed, was there no reason to fear that some might feel themselves called to subvert this system of wrong, by whatever means? From the free colored people this danger was particularly to be apprehended.

It is easy for us to place ourselves in their situation. Suppose that millions of white men were enslaved, robbed of all their rights, in a neighbouring country, and enslaved by a black race, who had torn their ancestors from the shores on which our fathers had lived. How deeply should we feel their wrongs! And would it be wonderful, if, in a moment of passionate excitement, some enthusiast should think it his duty to use his communication with his injured brethren for stirring them up to revolt?

Such is the danger from Abolitionism to the Slaveholding States. I know no other. It is but justice to add, that the principle of non-resistance, which the Abolitionists have connected with their passionate appeals, seems to have counteracted the peril. I know not a case in which a member of an anti-slavery society has been proved by legal investigation to have tampered with the slaves; and, after the strongly pronounced and unanimous opinion of the Free States on the subject, this danger may be considered as having passed away. Still a mode of action requiring these checks is open to strong objections, and ought to be abandoned. Happy will it be, if the disapprobation of friends, as well as of foes, should give to Abolitionists a caution and moderation, which would secure the acquiescence of the judicious, and the sympathies of the friends of mankind! Let not a good cause find its chief obstruction in its defenders. Let the truth, and the whole truth, be spoken without paltering or fear; but so spoken as to convince, not inflame, as to give no alarm to the wise, and no needless exasperation to the selfish and passionate.

I know it is said, that nothing can be done but by excitement and vehemence; that the zeal which dares every thing is the only power to oppose to long-rooted abuses. But it is not true that God has committed the great work of reforming the world to passion. Love is a minister of good, only when it gives energy to the intellect, and allies itself with wisdom. The Abolitionists often speak of Luther's vehemence as a model to future reformers. But who, that has read history, does not know, that Luther's reformation was accompanied by tremendous miseries and crimes, and that its progress was soon arrested? And is there not reason to fear, that the fierce, bitter, persecuting spirit, which he breathed into the work, not only tarnished its glory, but limited its power? One great principle, which we should lay down as immovably true, is, that, if a good work cannot be carried on by the calm, self-controlled, benevolent spirit of Christianity, then the time for doing it has not come. God asks not the aid of our vices. He can overrule them for good, but they are not the chosen instruments of human happiness. . . .

In lamenting the adoption by the Abolitionists of the system of agitation or extensive excitement, I do not mean to condemn this mode of action as only evil. There are cases to which it is adapted; and, in general, the impulse which it gives is better than the selfish, sluggish indifference to good objects, into which the multitude so generally fall. But it must not supersede or be compared with Individual action. The enthusiasm of the Individual in a good cause is a mighty power. The forced, artificially excited enthusiasm of a multitude, kept together by an organization which makes them the instruments of a few leading minds, works superficially, and often injuriously. I fear that the native, nobleminded enthusiast often loses that single-heartedness which is his greatest power, when once he strives to avail himself of the machinery of associations. . . .

The adoption of the common system of agitation by the Abolitionists has not been justified by success. From the beginning it created alarm in the considerate, and strengthened the sympathies of the Free States with the slave-holder. It made converts of a few individuals, but alienated multitudes. Its influence at the South has been almost wholly evil. It has stirred up bitter passions and a fierce fanaticism, which have shut every ear and every heart against its arguments and persuasions. These effects are more to be deplored, because the hope of freedom to the slave lies chiefly in the dispositions of his master. The Abolitionist proposed, indeed, to convert the slave-holders; and for this end he approached them with vituperation, and exhausted on them the vocabulary of reproach. And he has reaped as he sowed. His vehement pleadings for the slaves have been answered by wilder tones from the slaveholder; and, what is worse, deliberate defences of slavery have been sent forth, in the spirit of the dark ages, and in defiance of the moral convictions and feelings of the Christian and civilized world. Thus, with good purposes, nothing seems to have been gained. Perhaps (though I am anxious to repel the thought) something has been lost to the cause of freedom and humanity.

I earnestly desire that Abolitionism may lay aside the form of public agitation, and seek its end by wiser and milder means. I desire as earnestly, and more earnestly, that it may not be put down by Lawless Force. There is a worse evil than Abolitionism, and that is the suppression of it by lawless force. No evil greater than this can exist in the state, and this is never needed. Be it granted, that it is the design, or direct, palpable tendency of Abolitionism to stir up insurrection at the South, and that no existing laws can meet the exigency. It is the solemn duty of the chief magistrate of the state to assemble immediately the legislative bodies, and their duty immediately to apply the remedy of Law. Let every friend of freedom, let every good man lift up his voice against mobs. Through these lies our road to tyranny. . . .[2]

[2] From *The Works of William E. Channing* (Boston, 1849), II, 123–33.

16
The Southern Response

The reaction to Garrison in the South is of great histor-ical importance—not because, as the traditional historiography would have it, it resulted in the conversion of the South to the idea that slavery was "a positive good" (the commitment that was the basis for this affirmation existed before Garrison began his attack), but because it helped bring the South's militant defense of the institution out into the open in a way that aroused North-ern fears and anxieties.

The emotional intensity of the initial Southern response is re-flected in the following two letters received by Garrison in 1832 and printed in the Liberator *for January 28 and March 31.*

Athens, (Geo.) Jan. 10th, 1832

To the Editor of the Liberator.

With the utmost astonishment and indignation, sir, I have read one of the late numbers of this most slanderous and villainous publication. With the utmost stretch of my imagination, I never could have con-ceived of a man so absolutely destitute of every patriotic principle, as in the open blaze of day thus to disseminate doctrines and principles so entirely at variance with the peace, happiness and prosperity, nay the very existence of the Republic. You undoubtedly, sir, have reflected upon what you are doing. For the life that's in me I cannot conceive what your object can be, unless it be to destroy that free and happy government under which we now live. You cannot expect, by these base and impudent *lies* which you are circulating to benefit the slaves —Impossible. You cannot expect to render your countrymen better, wiser or happier; nor can you expect service whether to God or man. Your motives, then, must be unholy, illegal, unjustifiable emolument, or to destroy the peace and harmony of the country. Instead of melio-rating the condition of the slaves, you are rendering them ten-fold more wretched, thus adding their misery to the catalogue of your black, daring and unchristian deeds. Look at the effects already produced by the circulation of your abominable paper in different parts of the South. How many innocent women and children have been hurried from the stage of being by the lawless hands of these African desperadoes, whose minds have been inflamed and wrought up to the utmost pitch of madness by the principles propagated through your diabolical agency, and that of your infernal satellites—all emissaries of him who is "going about as a roaring lion, seeking whom he may devour." But your work of death and carnage stops not there. These same slaves, whom you profess to benefit, are necessarily, and as a matter of course, for their daring atrocities, put to the most painful and miserable death. And indeed the slaves generally throughout the country, who have not put their fell designs into execution, are treated by their masters with greater rigor than they would be, did not this excitement exist. But I suppose you congratulate yourself in being so happy as to bring about this state of things. Base villain! And you can look with complacency and delight upon the sufferings of your fellow-men, when you will know they can result in no good to any living creature? Such fiend-like barbarity, such infernal wickedness, is enough to chill the blood of the veriest monster that ever breathed the vital air. The sole object of your paper seems to be to drive the slaves to open and indiscriminate rebellion, when you are just as absolutely certain that they can never obtain their freedom in that way, as you are of your own abominable infamy. If your only desire was the abolition of slavery in this country, you would take up the subject calmly and dispassionately, and reason upon it, endeavor to convince, to persuade, and offer some means by which we could rid ourselves of the burden. I myself, sir, would become a subscriber to your paper, give up all my slaves, and use the best of my endeavors to push forward the success of the cause, while thousands of voices from the South would respond a hearty amen to every suggestion that might promise the accomplishment of the desired end. We are in principle as much opposed to slavery as your honorable self; it is an evil, and it is one which we must mildly endure, until we can rid ourselves of it in a suitable manner. Suggest a plan, sir, and see if we do not embrace it. But no—you will write it out of the country; you speak, and it must be done; you will thunder it out by the potency of your gigantic arm; by one blast of your tremendous artillery, you will blow it into oblivion. You impudent scoundrel! And I will blow you where the buzzards will never find you. Meet me, sir, in Washington City, on the 4th day of March, prepared

to meet the fate which you so richly deserve. Write me whether or not
you accept this challenge; if not, sir, expect to die in at least one
month thereafter, either by my one own arm or that of the state. For
be assured, sir, that if you continue your publication, you will be
officially demanded; and when the state calls you must, you shall come.
I now ask you, will you desist? or shall I be compelled to ride more
than 1000 miles to put a period to the rascality of so base, infamous,
abominable, traitorous, lawless, unprincipled, impudent, degraded,
cowardly a dog as you are?

A SLAVEHOLDER
Athens, Geo.[1]

To Wm. Lloyd Garrison:

There has been accidentally thrown in my way a paper headed "The
Liberator." The beautiful cuts with which it is decorated, attracted
my attention, and induced me to peruse its contents. Your paper, Sir,
is a lame and impotent production, designed obviously for the most
base and infamous purpose; and can have no other ultimate effect than
to render the negroes dissatisfied with their condition, and thereby
make it necessary to hold them in stricter subjection. If you were not
actuated by some dark and malignant motive, you would not oppose
the Colonization Society because its means of removing an evil are
not commensurate with the extent of that evil. It is evident to every
man of common sense who ever resided six months south of the
Potowmack, that the liberation of our slaves cannot be borne, unless
followed by speedy emigration. Slavery is admitted by all to be an
evil—repugnant to our interests as well as to our principles; but the
existence of free negroes amongst us not only increases the evil, but is
itself an evil of still greater magnitude. The free negro population
with us are generally and almost universally lazy, worthless, im-
provident and vicious in the extreme. The misdemeanors of the slaves
are in nine cases out of ten, plainly attributable to their influence.
What is the condition of the slaves? You represent them to be a degraded, heartbroken race, treated in the most barbarous manner by
their relentless and remorseless masters. You are ignorant of the fact,
or you lie like a rascal. In either case, it is presumption in you to
undertake to inform the public on the subject. I assert and defy contradiction, that ninety-nine slaveholders out of one hundred, treat

---

[1] From the *Liberator* (Boston), January 28, 1832.

their slaves not only with humanity, but with kindness and partiality; furnishing them with comfortable houses, abundant fuel, good clothing, wholesome and plentiful diet, and often with indulgences that many freemen in any country would be glad to enjoy. On the other hand, all that is required of them is moderate labor, mostly yielding no more than would pay their tax, support themselves and families, and pay the rent of the land if they were free. The poor white man, after suffering anxiety, suggesting means, and straining every muscle, can do no more in this part of the country. From whence, then, arises your opposition to the Colonization Society? Does it propose to carry any to Liberia against their will? Is not the constitution of the negro particularly adapted to the climate? Is it not the land from whence they sprang—the home of their ancestors? If the Society cannot remove all, they can remove a portion; and however few, they are benefitted and their posterity to the latest generation. The hopes of the philanthropist, and of every friend to the negro, must centre in this object, and their exertions must be united in this plan. Every other attempt to ameliorate their condition, must prove not only useless and abortive, but absolutely pernicious, by instilling into them notions of privileges they can never enjoy here, and exciting hopes they can never realize. If you could liberate them, Mr. Liberator, what would you do with them? The blacks and whites cannot assimilate: one must be subordinate to the other: we must control them, or submit to their control. Entire separation is the only method of securing to them political rights. I repeat, your publications have only the tendency to render the slaves discontented, and to foster the prejudices of the north against the customs and institutions of the south. You ask with great self-complacency, if the slaves are uninstructed, how can they be apprized of your seditious publications? You know very well, that your fanatical party are not wanting in agents, who, having found peddling unprofitable, have taken to preaching; and who, under the pretext of taking care of their "immortal souls," are endeavoring to lead them on to privy conspiracy and rebellion. They require no learning to exaggerate and communicate your unprincipled suggestions and hell-engendered doctrines thus introduced, from one to another. You may be assured that the more you attempt to wrest them from us, the stronger will be our grasp; and if they succeed for a moment in loosing their bonds, it must only be to submit to those which are more firm. We hold them in self defence; let them alone, or take them entirely from us. Take notice that I speak of bonds in a figurative sense; your assertion that we have them literally bound—fettered—manacled—is too glaring a falsehood to gain credence any where.

There is another small matter between us, Master Garrison. You don't seem to like the law of your State, which prohibits the unholy alliance between white and black. Suppose you were to take a fancy to a brute; would you not make the same objections to the law against Sodomy? Answer me that, Master Garrison. The white man or woman who would consent to marry a negro, deserves to be hung with a knotty grape vine, without benefit of Clergy. "Fleas are not Lobsters— d—n their souls." Negroes and white men are essentially distinct in their nature. It is a most odious and odorous comparison. The dark complexion, peculiar features, woolly hair and small skulls of the negroes, are not their only characteristics. Their blood is not of the temperature of ours by two degrees; and their mental capacities are an hundred degrees below that of their white "brethren," as you are pleased to call us. It is idle to take the intelligence of a few individuals, as a criterion by which to judge of their intellect as a people. Such instances only serve to unite these two links in the chain of creation, which extends from the honorable, freeborn, highbred Virginian, down to the meanest reptile in existence, such as your ignoble self. The progeny of a Yankee and Negro would indeed be a nondescript in natural history; uniting the selfishness, duplicity, canting hypocrisy and vicious propensities of the one, to the recklessness, obstinacy and folly of the other: in short, just such a monster as yourself. Publish this without mutilation or alteration. I dare you. Answer me without equivocation or evasion. I defy you. And if your infamous and villainous paper should ever again pollute my sight, I'll publish you from Dan to Beersheba, until you cry "hold, enough."

HOTSPUR.[2]

In the following excerpt, Garrison is attacked in the typical Southern fashion of the mid-1830's by William Drayton, a South Carolina apologist for slavery.

But a few years have elapsed since the commencement of the abolition movement. It originated in a few heated and disturbed minds,

[2] From the *Liberator* (Boston), March 31, 1832.

and was urged in the face of every obstacle. Wm. Lloyd Garrison, Lundy, and some others, who conceived themselves the chosen instruments of accomplishing abolition, proclaimed their peculiar doctrines with an ardour, which, if it did not excite respect, at least attracted attention. Garrison, the most talented and rabid of the corps, soon became notorious. In the fury of his zeal he did not scruple to borrow the aid of fiction; and, at times, indulged his talent for invective, at the expense of truth, and of the character of respectable citizens. The difficulties into which this unfortunate propensity plunged him, only excited his ardour anew. The strict confinement and low diet to which the irreverend administrators of the law consigned him, did not allay the violence of his zeal. He regarded his misfortune as a partial martyrdom. It certainly had one advantage—it lifted him to an elevation which, like that of the pillory, rendered him the observed of all observers. He renewed his denunciations with spirit. He raved, and the world laughed; but in the end he proved that, so ricketty and unstable a thing is the world, even the efforts of a madman can disturb it. He gained disciples—what fanatic ever raved without converts?—and soon became an object of attention to the crack-brained enthusiasts and antiquated ladies of the whole land. The Colonization Society had, by agitating the subject, prepared the country for the coming of this second Peter the Hermit; and the crusade preached by him against the institutions of the South, found supporters and advocates. At length, he enlisted a sufficient force in behalf of abolition, to enable him to visit England, and crave foreign influence against the laws and lives of his fellow countrymen. England was herself reeling under the potions of quacks and enthusiasts, and lent a willing ear to the crazed abstractions, wild appeals, and exaggerated statements, of Garrison. He found himself in his element. He preached against his country to applauding multitudes; he denounced Washington as a robber, because a slave-holder; characterized the American Constitution as a guilty and blood-stained instrument, because it recognized the domestic laws of the South; and, in short, indulged, to his heart's content, in foul and frothy invective against all that is dear and sacred to Americans. Having sufficiently blackened his country abroad, he returned to renew his treasonable efforts at home. He was received by the fanatics with rapture; and the work was resumed with fresh ardour. The efforts of these conspirators, at their midnight meetings, where the bubbling cauldron of abolition was filled with its pestilential materials, and the fire beneath kindled by the breath

of the fanatics, has often reminded us of the witch scene in Macbeth.
Their chorus is peculiarly in character for the amalgamationists.

"Black spirits and white,
Red spirits and gray,
Mingle, mingle, mingle,
You that mingle may."

It requires no excited imagination to conceive them gathered in their
secret councils, where, at first, a few half-crazed enthusiasts, with a
bevy of female fanatics, met to hatch and prepare this precious scheme.
In such a conclave, assembled for such a purpose, the incantation of
the scene referred to, would have been wholly appropriate.

"For a charm of powerful trouble,
Like a hell-broth, boil and bubble.
Double, double, toil and trouble,
Fire burn and cauldron bubble!"

In these scenes we may suppose that Garrison, gloomy, wild, and
malignant, was the ruling spirit. His religious madness, his vehement
cant and violence of spirit naturally gained for him the mastery in
their councils. Whatever may be the character of his coadjutors, Garrison has, in his whole career, betrayed the worst purposes allied to the
worst passions. His writings have been blackened with the vilest
slanders, and the most vindictive abuse. Indeed, so vehement, rancorous and fiend-like have been his exhibitions of passion against his
opponents, that most persons have considered, and do still consider,
him insane. It is a probable and certainly a charitable supposition; for
if he is to be considered as strictly accountable for his ravings, he
must be held in general execration. The following extract from his
writings is a specimen of his style, and certainly affords no evidence
of the soundness of either his head or his heart. He addresses the
slave-holders. The reader will be reminded of the celebrated sermon of
Maw-worm.

Ye crafty calculators! Ye hard-hearted incorrigible sinners! Ye greedy
and relentless robbers! Ye contemners of justice and mercy! Ye trembling, pitiful, pale-faced usurpers! My soul spurns you with unspeakable
disgust!

The style of Garrison is turgid, but often effective. His compositions appear intended to operate principally upon the ignorant blacks; and are filled with declamation, denunciation and cant. In abusing his opponents, he exhibits a frantic and frontless disregard of the decencies of the press. In advocating his doctrines, he pauses at no difficulty. If good men sanction slavery—they are robbers; if the Constitution maintains it—it must be crushed; if the Union is an obstacle—it must be overthrown. He never writes without raving; he even reasons like a bedlamite; and in his paper, which has great influence over the blacks, he has done much to excite a spirit of insubordination and violence.

Until recently, these outrages were allowed to pass unpunished; but the time has at length arrived when a wronged and insulted people will no longer permit these madmen to tamper with the peace and welfare of our country. The citizens of Boston recently took possession of the person of Garrison, with a view to summary punishment, and were only deterred by compassion, from bestowing on him the honorary ointment and robe which has, time immemorial, been decreed in the East to traitors. He was, however, committed to prison as a protection from the just indignation of the people, and in the morning escaped from the city in disguise.[3]

As the years passed, the South saw no reason to change its opinion of Garrison, who remained the archetype of the dangerous Northern fanatic. One of the most extreme defenders of slavery was George Fitzhugh of Virginia, a writer who was willing to attack the very notion of a free society. In his book Cannibals All, *published in 1857, Fitzhugh describes Garrison as the leading Northern radical. In the same passage, he also mentions Charles Lenox Remond, a Negro abolitionist, Theodore Parker, the radical Unitarian minister, and Stephen Pearl Andrews, the anarchist. In representing these men as all speaking at the same meeting, Fitzhugh suggests a more tightly organized radical "conspiracy" than in fact existed.*

Mr. Garrison . . . heads the extreme wing of the Socialist, Infidel, Woman's-Right, Agrarian and Abolition party, who are called

[3] From [William Drayton], *The South Vindicated from the Treason and Fanaticism of the Northern Abolitionists* (Philadelphia, 1835), pp. 157–60.

Garrisonians. He edits the *Liberator,* which is conducted with an ability worthy of a better cause. He and his followers seem to admit that the Bible and the Constitution recognize and guarantee Slavery, and therefore denounce both, and propose disunion and no priests or churches as measures to attain abolition. Mr. Garrison usually presides at their meetings, and we infer, in part, their principles and doctrines, from the materials that compose those meetings. A Wise-Woman will rise and utter a philippic against Marriage, the Bible, and the Constitution—and will be followed by negro Remond, who "spits upon Washington," and complains of the invidious distinction of calling whites Anglo-Saxons, and negroes Africans. And now, Phillips arises,

> Armed with hell-flames and fury,

and gently begins, in tones more dulcet, and with action more graceful than Belial, to

> Pour the sweet milk of concord into hell!
> Uproar the universal peace—
> Destroy all unity on earth.

Then Mr. Parker will edify the meeting by stirring up to bloody deeds in Kansas or in Boston—in which, as becomes his cloth, he takes no part—and ends by denouncing things in general, and the churches and parsons in particular. And, probably, the whole will conclude with a general indulgence and remission of sins, from Mr. Andrews, who assumes, for the nonce, the character of Father Confessor, and assures the tender conscience that it is right and incumbent to take the oath to sustain the Constitution with the deliberate purpose of violating it, because such oaths are taken under moral duress. These Garrisonians are as intellectual men as any in the nation. They lead the Black Republican party, and control the politicians. Yet are they deadly enemies of Northern as well as of Southern institutions.

Now, gentlemen, all of you are philosophers, and most zealous philanthropists, and have for years been roaring, at the top of your voice, to the Oi Polloi rats, that the old crazy edifice of society, in which they live, is no longer fit for human dwelling, and is imminently dangerous. The rats have taken you at your word, and are rushing headlong, with the haste and panic of a *sauve qui peut,* into every hole that promises shelter—into "any port in a storm." Some join the Rappists and Shakers; thousands find a temporary shelter in Mr. Greeley's Fourierite Phalansteries; many more follow Mr. Andrews to Trialville, to villages in the far West, or to Modern Times; and a select few to the saloons of Free Love; and hundreds of thousands find shelter with Brigham Young, in Utah; whilst others, still more frightened, go to consult the Spiritual Telegraph, that raps hourly at the doors of heaven and of hell, or quietly put on their ascension robes to accompany Parson Miller in his upward flight. But the greater number are waiting (very impatiently) for Mr. Andrews to establish his New and Better World, or for Mr. Garrison and Mr. Goodell to inaugurate their Millennium.

Why, Gentlemen! none of these worse than Cassandra vaticinations —why none of this panic, terror, confusion, and flight in Slave Society? Are we suffering, and yet contented? Is our house tumbling about our heads, and we sitting in conscious security amidst the impending ruin? No! No! Our edifice is one that never did fall, and never will fall; for Nature's plastic hand reared it, supports it, and will forever sustain it.

Have we not shown, in this single chapter, that the North has as much to apprehend from abolition as the South, and that it is time for conservatives everywhere to unite in efforts to suppress and extinguish it? [4]

[4] From George Fitzhugh, *Cannibals All! Or Slaves Without Masters*, ed. C. Vann Woodward (Cambridge, Mass., 1960), pp. 95–97. Reprinted by permission of the Belknap Press of Harvard University Press.

17
Northern Conservative Reactions

Garrison was not very popular in the North, as the Boston mob incident would suggest. In May, 1850, Garrison was mobbed again, this time in New York City at the annual meeting of the American Anti-Slavery Society. The actual work of harassing the speakers and breaking up the meeting was carried out by a gang of toughs under the leadership of Captain Isaiah Rynders. But behind Rynders and his followers was a substantial body of aroused anti-abolitionist opinion. The following selection is from an editorial which appeared in the New York Herald, *a leading Democratic paper, on the opening day of the convention.*

What these abolitionists want has been fully explained by the squandered wisdom of [Horace] Greeley, [Albert] Brisbane, Garrison, [Richard Henry] Dana, Abby Kelly, and Wen[dell] Phillips, with their coadjutors in social disturbances and aggressions upon the rational conventions, and usages, and wholesome laws of society.

Sixteen years ago, Garrison, during Thurlow Weed's anti-masonic excitement, (which was the first platform of Seward), became ambitious of political distinction. He found slavery a good hobby to ride upon, and throwing off something of his clerical reserve, he sought martyr-dom. In this he was disappointed. However, he went on from step to step, til the World's Convention of 1840, when he and his compatriots quarrelled with the churches of this country; and since then he has boldly urged the utter overthrow of the churches, the Sabbath, and the Bible. Nothing has been sacred with him but the ideal intellect of the negro race. To elevate this chimera, he has urged the necessity of an immediate overthrow of the government, a total disrespect for the Constitution, actual disruption and annihilation of the Union, and the cessation of all order, legal and divine, which does not square with his narrow views of what constitutes human liberty. Never, in the time of the French revolution and blasphemous atheism, was there more malevolence and unabashed wickedness avowed than by this same Garrison. Indeed, he surpasses Robespierre and his associates, for he has no design of building up. His only object is to destroy. In sixteen years he has done something. He has worked upon the political parties of the time, gaining something but acknowledging nothing and maintaining an entire destruction of the great interests of the country to be essential to the cause of birth in liberty. In this view of his chimerical doctrines, he has brought around him such men and women to aid him, as we have noticed, and many of these, such as Parker Pillsbury, Theodore Parker, and Abby Folsom, have entertained his political creed, and have even avowed, like him, that the Sabbath should be blocked out of the calendar. In Boston, a few months ago, a convention was held, the object of which was the overthrow of Sunday worship.

Thus, it appears that nothing divine or secular is respected by these fanatics. They have only in view utter annihilation of all the great and sacred interests of society. They would array in dreadful hostility one section of the Union against the other, and stop the wheels of government by their insane agitation—malcontents who find nothing honest but their own honesty, nothing sacred but their own divinity, nothing liberal but their own illiberality, to the elevation and diffusion of which, all their time, talents and opportunities are directed, for no good, but for the ultimate detriment of every race, and the cause of liberty throughout the world.

When free discussion does not promote the public good, it has no more right to exist than a bad government, that is dangerous and oppressive to the common weal. It should be overthrown. On the question of usefulness to the public, of the packed, organized meetings of these abolitionists, socialists, Sabbath breakers and anarchists, there can be but one result arrived at by prudence and patriotism. They are dangerous assemblies—calculated for mischief, and treasonable in their character and purposes. Though the law cannot reach them, public opinion can; and, as in England a peaceful dissent from such doctrines as these fellows would promulgate—a strong expression of dissent from them—would be conveyed by hisses and counter statements and expositions, so here in New York we would anticipate that there are those who will enter the arena of discussion, and send out the true opinion of the public. That half a dozen madmen should manufacture opinion for the whole community is not to be tolerated. It is to be hoped, that before long, we shall learn what public opinion upon the Union, truly is—and what interest all the masses have in the perpetuity of the Sabbath and our institutions.[1]

Even in 1860, when antislavery sentiment had risen to new heights as the result of events of the previous decade, Garrison remained a controversial figure whose philosophy and behavior were openly endorsed by few Northerners. Leaders of the Free-Soil movement, which had become institutionalized in the Republican Party, disavowed any connection with the Garrisonian abolitionists. But their Northern opponents, following the lead of Southerners like Fitzhugh, persisted in accusing them of being spiritually in league with the abolitionists, whether they admitted it or not. The following description of a speech by Garrison, headlined "Wm. Lloyd Garrison at City Hall," is from the conservative Lawrence (Massachusetts) Sentinel of July 7, 1860.

This notorious agitator and skeptic held forth at City Hall, last Sabbath, in defense of his peculiar views. Large audiences were present.

In the afternoon he descanted upon the Bible, denying its authenticity and inspiration, and claiming that it should be accepted as truth only in so far as it accorded with the opinions of the individual. The discourse, though marked by considerable ability, accredited its author as the possessor of an erratic and unbalanced mind.

But the evening lecture was *the* feature of his performance. Slavery was his topic, and he fulfilled his promise to unfold the character of Garrisonian Abolitionism. He claimed with truth that his principles were identical with those of the Republicans, the only point of difference being that *he* boldly followed out Republican ideas to their logical conclusion, while *they* timidly shrank therefrom. He conceded that the indignities offered their opposition to slavery, were occasioned by the agitation on "higher law" grounds, arguing that slavery being wrong, it was a duty to eradicate it, regardless of consequences. He threw a bomb-shell into the Republican ranks when he said that if slaves were rightfully held as property in the States, they were held with parity of right in the Territories.

The whole lecture was of the "fire-eating" order, after the fashion of the *Liberator,* and disgusting to all right-thinking and loyal citizens. He advocated the utopian and fatal idea of immediate emancipation

[1] From *New York Herald,* May 7, 1850.

—an idea impossible in itself, and were it possible, full of disaster to the white and black alike. The Union he looked upon as "a covenant with death and an agreement with hell," and prayed for its dissolution. Slaveholders were abused with more violence and vulgarity than were exhibited in Sumner's defamatory oration, and all "doughfaces" were severely flagellated. To our minds exhibitions of this sort on the Sabbath are improper and disgraceful. . . . The large majority of those who met to listen to Garrison . . . went in the same spirit as they would visit a theatre or other place of amusement. . . . We would not interfere with Mr. Garrison in the expression of his vagaries. They are so violent and extravagant, that in an intelligent community no harm can come of them. But in the name of a decent propriety we protest against the use of the Sabbath for such public performances as were transacted in our City Hall last Sunday evening.[2]

[2] Reprinted in the *Liberator* (Boston), July 20, 1860.

18

Harriet Martineau: An English Radical Describes a Meeting with Garrison[1]

One of the best personal glimpses of Garrison was provided by Harriet Martineau, an English reformer, who met Garrison in 1835, shortly after he had been mobbed in Boston.

I was staying at the house of a clergyman in Boston, when a note was brought in which told me that Mr. Garrison was in town, and would meet me at any hour, at any friend's house, the next day. My host arrived at a knowledge of the contents of the note quite against my will, and kindly insisted that Mr. Garrison should call on me at home. At ten o'clock he came, accompanied by his introducer. His aspect put to flight in an instant what prejudices his slanderers had raised in me. I was wholly taken by surprise. It was a countenance glowing with health, and wholly expressive of purity, animation, and gentleness. I did not now wonder at the citizen who, seeing a print of Garrison at a shop window without a name to it, went in and bought it, and framed it as the most saintlike of countenances. The end of the story is, that when the citizen found whose portrait he had been hanging up in his parlor, he took the print out of the frame and huddled it away.

Garrison has a good deal of a Quaker air; and his speech is deliberate like a Quaker's, but gentle as a woman's. The only thing that I did not like was his excessive agitation when he came in, and his thanks to me for desiring to meet one "so odious" as himself. I was, however, as I told him, nearly as odious as himself at that time; so it was fit that we should be acquainted. On mentioning afterward to his introducer my impression of something like a want of manliness

[1] From Harriet Martineau, *Retrospect of Western Travel,* as reprinted in W. P. Garrison and F. J. Garrison, *Life,* II, 69–71.

in Garrison's agitation, he replied that I could not know what it was to be an object of insult and hatred to the whole of society for a series of years; that Garrison could bear what he met with from street to street, and from town to town; but that a kind look and shake of the hand from a stranger unmanned him for the moment. How little did the great man know our feelings towards him on our meeting; how we, who had done next to nothing, were looking up to him who is achieving the work of an age, and, as a stimulus, that of a nation!

His conversation was more about peace principles than the great subject. It was of the most practical cast. Every conversation I had with him confirmed my opinion that sagacity is the most striking attribute of his conversation. It has none of the severity, the harshness, the bad taste of his writing; it is as gladsome as his countenance, and as gentle as his voice. Through the whole of his deportment breathes the evidence of a heart at ease; and this it is, I think, more than all his distinct claims, which attaches his personal friends to him with an almost idolatrous affection.

* * *

I do not pretend to like or to approve the tone of Garrison's printed censures. I could not use such language myself towards any class of offenders, nor can I sympathize in its use by others. But it is only fair to mention that Garrison adopts it warily; and that I am persuaded that he is elevated above passion, and has no unrighteous anger to vent in harsh expressions. He considers his task to be the exposure of fallacy, the denunciation of hypocrisy, and the rebuke of selfish timidity. He is looked upon by those who defend him in this particular as holding the branding-iron; and it seems true enough that no one branded by Garrison ever recovers from it. He gives his reasons for his severity with a calmness, meekness, and softness which contrast strongly with the subject of the discourse, and which convince the objector that there is principle at the bottom of the practice. . . .

He never speaks of himself or his persecutions unless compelled, and his child will never learn at home what a distinguished father he has. He will know him as the tenderest of parents before he becomes aware that he is a great hero. I found myself growing into a forgetfulness of the deliverer of a race in the friend of the fireside. One day, in Michigan, two friends (who happened to be abolitionists) and I were taking a drive with the Governor of the State, who was talking of some recent commotion on the slavery question. "What is Garrison like?" said he. "Ask Miss M.," said one smiling friend: "Ask Miss M.," said the other. I was asked accordingly; and my answer was, that I thought Garrison the most bewitching personage I had met in the United States. The impression cannot but be strengthened by his being made such a bugbear as he is; but the testimony of his personal friends, the closest watchers of his life, may safely be appealed to as to the charms of his domestic manners.

Garrison gayly promised me that he would come over whenever his work is done in the United States, that we may keep jubilee in London. I believe it would be safe to promise him a hundred thousand welcomes as warm as mine.

PART THREE

GARRISON
IN HISTORY

19
Henry Wilson (1873)[1]

The most ambitious historical account of the struggle against slavery written by a Northern participant was Henry Wilson's History of the Rise and Fall of the Slave Power. Wilson, a long-time Republican Senator from Massachusetts, was elected Vice President of the United States in 1872. His account is of interest because it praises Garrison for his courage and high ideals but suggests that he was too radical to have had much influence in the ante-bellum North. Wilson's testimony on this point is significant because he himself was a product of the wider anti-slavery consciousness that grew up in the 1850's independently of Garrison and the radical abolitionists.

Mr. Garrison's partner in the publication of "The Liberator" was Mr. Isaac Knapp, a printer, like himself, and also a native of the same town. The paper was commenced without funds and without a single subscriber. Bearing the comprehensive and cosmopolitan motto, "My country is the world, my countrymen are all mankind," it appealed to no party, sect, or interest for recognition and support. Both editor and printer labored hard and fared meagrely; and it was only thus—and a marvel it was at that—that their journal lived. But Mr. Garrison had a mission to fulfil, and he bravely met the conditions it imposed. For, whatever may be the estimate of his policy, and whatever may have been his mistakes, none can withhold the meed of admiration at the moral courage and faith he exhibited as he entered

[1] From Henry Wilson, *The History of the Rise and Fall of the Slave Power in America* (Boston, 1873), I, 184–88.

upon his life's work. Hardly grander were their exhibition when Kepler was working out his problem of the solar system, willing to "wait a century for a reader"; when Columbus was travelling through Europe, from court to court, from philosopher to prince, in the vain search for a convert to his new theory of a western passage to the Indies; or even when Luther was nailing his theses to the door of the church, and thus braving the thunders of the Vatican, than when that young man—with no advantages of birth or culture, with wounds still bleeding from his recent encounter with the dark and bloody tyrant, in his dingy room of sixteen feet square, at once his sanctum, workshop, and home—made assault upon a despotism which not only trampled millions of slaves in the dust, but dominated the whole country, binding both church and state in chains, and there forged his weapons of warfare from the indestructible materials of God's Word and the Declaration of Independence. It must have been something more than "the grace of indignation" which urged him on, which crowned him with the honors of imprisonment, gave him the garland of a rope, the escort of a mob of Boston's "respectability and standing," and extorted such honorable mention by Southern governors and legislatures as can now be gathered from their records.

It was not that Mr. Garrison discovered any new truths, or that he stood alone, which gave him his prominence from the start. The sinfulness of slaveholding and the duty of its immediate relinquishment had been as unequivocally proclaimed by others, and there were those then in the field as decided and pronounced as he. It must have arisen partly, at least, from the peculiar state of public opinion at that time. After the crowning triumph of the Slave Power in the Missouri Compromise, and in the sectional victory of the South, by the defeat of Mr. Adams and the election of General Jackson, there seemed to be a general acquiescence on the part of the people in these triumphs, and a growing disposition to remit further antislavery effort.

The nation had reached its nadir; for, though there were subsequently other aggressions, more flagrant outrages, and new concessions and compromises, yet never after that was the nation so voiceless and timid. Cowed and silent before the domineering Power, with the number of protestants growing fewer and feebler, the very boldness and seeming audacity of the young man in his attic, telling the nation that he was in earnest and would be heard, aroused attention. The very deliberation with which he heralded and began the assault, the stern defiance he bade the foe at whose feet he threw the gauntlet of mortal combat, made him the mark for criticism and hostile demonstration, as well as the rallying point of those who sympathized with him in spirit and in purpose. His impartiality, too, between sects and parties, men and schools, constitutions and laws, and whatever arrayed itself against the slave or remained neutral, increased that attention and criticism.

His pen, if possible, was more severe, caustic, and exasperating than had been his speech. While friends generally doubted and questioned, and the people condemned, the slaveholders were stung to madness. Before the close of the first year, the Vigilance Association of Columbia, South Carolina, "composed of gentlemen of the first respectability," offered a reward of fifteen hundred dollars for the apprehension and conviction of any white person detected in circulating in that State "the newspaper called 'The Liberator.'" The corporation of Georgetown, in the District of Columbia, passed an ordinance rendering it penal for any free person of color to take from the post-office "the paper published in Boston called 'The Liberator,'" the punishment for each offence to be twenty dollars' fine or thirty days' imprisonment. In case the offender was not able to pay the fine, or the fees for imprisonment, he was to be sold into slavery for four months. The grand jury of Raleigh, North Carolina, at the instigation of the attorney-general, made an indictment against the editor and publisher of "The Liberator" for its circulation in that county. The legislature of Georgia proceeded to pass an act, which was promptly signed by Governor Lumpkin, offering a reward of five thousand dollars for the arrest, prosecution, and trial to conviction, under the laws of the State, of the editor or publisher "of a certain paper called 'The Liberator,' published in the town of Boston and State of Massachusetts."

But neither the doubts of friends, the condemnation of the North, nor the threats and offered rewards of the South, moved Mr. Garrison from his purpose. He bade defiance to his persecutors, and avowed his readiness to die, if need be. He stood, he says, "like the oak, like the Alps,—unshaken, storm-proof. Opposition and abuse and slander and prejudice and judicial tyranny add to the flame of my zeal. I am not discouraged; I am not dismayed; but bolder and more confident than ever."

Nor is there any doubt that his voice and pen were among the most potent influences that produced the antislavery revival of that day. Antislavery societies were formed, antislavery presses were established, and antislavery lectures abounded. Nine years after the establishment of "The Liberator" there were nearly two thousand antislavery societies, with a membership of some two hundred thousand. This result, however, was not secured without agitation, controversy, and strife. Nor were these all outside of the societies. Within them were discords and dissensions, growing out of the nature of their work and the character of their members. For the latter were generally, and almost of necessity, persons of positive convictions and self-assertion, engaged in a work of appalling magnitude and beset with unanticipated difficulties. Especially true was this of those who gathered around Mr. Garrison, adopted and defended his views, and recognized him as their leader. Embracing many men, and especially women, of talent, culture, and eloquence, they were a small, compact, aggressive, and somewhat destructive body, who, with marked characteristics and occasional idosyncrasies, yet seemed to be swayed by a common impulse, and to be committed not only to a common object, but to the pursuit of that object by modes peculiarly their own.

In pursuance of their object, they avowed the purpose of granting quarter to nothing which, in their apprehension, interposed itself between them and that object. Not finding that hearty co-operation and ready acquiescence in their utterances and modes of action in church or state which they desired or hoped for, but oftener hostility and persecution, they soon arrayed themselves in antagonism to the leading influences of both. And so, singularly enough, they presented what appeared to their countrymen the practical solecism of endeavoring to reform the government by renouncing all connection with it; of seeking to remove a political evil by refusing all association with political parties, by whose action alone that evil could be reached; of depending alone on moral suasion, and an appeal to the consciences of the people, and yet coming out of all the religious associations and assemblies of the land. This arraying themselves against the patriotism, the partisanship, and the religious sentiment of the great body of the people prevented harmonious co-operation, and rendered inevitable, sooner or later, a disruption of the national society. In that separation, which took place in 1840, but a small part remained with Mr. Garrison,—probably not more than one fifth of the members of the antislavery societies then existing; and these were confined mainly to New England, and mostly to Eastern Massachusetts. Nor did their numbers increase during the conflicts of the subsequent twenty years. Indeed, it is doubtful whether, in 1860, when Mr. Lincoln was elected by a vote of nearly two millions, on a clearly defined and distinct issue with the Slave Power, there were more Abolitionists of that school than there were twenty years before, when the American Antislavery Society was rent in twain. During all this period, however, they acted, as they professed, "without concealment and without compromise." Whatever may be the estimate of the weight of their influence on public opinion, none will ever doubt the sincerity of their convictions, the purity of their motives, the boldness of their utterances, or the inflexibility of their purposes.

20
James Schouler (1889)[1]

James Schouler, author of a multi-volumed history of the United States, was one of the first professional historians in the North who was, on the whole, antagonistic to Garrison and his followers. Schouler's account of Garrison as a dangerous radical who was at best a regrettable historical necessity reflects the ambivalence of many late nineteenth-century Northerners when confronting the record of abolitionist agitation. However necessary the abolitionists may have been in order to arouse the North on the subject of slavery, they were to be disparaged personally because of the bad precedent set by their behavior, and it is noteworthy that Schouler's figurative description of Garrison as a "bomb thrower" was published only three years after a real bomb allegedly had been thrown by radicals during the Haymarket riots in Chicago.

This new abolition movement at the North did not, like the Quaker one of former days, respect constitutional bounds and seek mild persuasion of the white master who held the local law in his hands. It boldly proclaimed that the laws of nature were paramount to a human institution; it preached freedom as of divine right and in defiance, if need be, of the enslaver. But in law-respecting communities like ours all such agitation bruised itself like a bird against the solid wall of the federal constitution, which, wisely or unwisely, surrounded the institution and sanctioned its existence within certain State confines. Antipathy to weaker men and races, and a dogged attachment to property as something with which none others are to interfere, save as their own property may be injured by it, are two strong traits of the Anglo-Saxon. He has a conscience, domestic virtue, and a restraining common sense to be influenced; but of woman herself Shakespeare's Petruchio talked like an Englishman rather than an

[1] From James Schouler, *History of the United States of America Under the Constitution* (New York, 1892), IV, 210–21. (Originally published in 1889.)

Italian of his day, when he said, "I will be master of what is mine own." And such was our slaveholder's response to the abolitionist when menaced where he stood. Pride and blind interest banded the southern masters in bristling defiance; patriots of all sections felt the constraint of the written law, and then abolitionism slid into an angry tirade against the constitution as a covenant with death and agreement with hell, and its creed became "no union with slaveholders,"—in a word, disunion, because instant and legalized abolition was impossible. We shall see in the angry years that follow southern secessionists and northern abolitionists standing upon essentially the same platform, though at opposite ends, both demanding that the American Union be broken up.

The boldest exponent of this new anti-slavery school, the pioneer and arch-agitator of immediate abolition, of conscience above the constitution, was William Lloyd Garrison. . . . With merciless severity, he arraigned the frozen apathy of the North and the prostitution of the South on the slavery question; he could not tolerate scruples on behalf of the written law; all doughfaces, apologists, and timeservers he wrote down as traitors and cowards, and unhesitatingly he declared slavery to be a crime and the slaveholder himself a criminal. "I am in earnest," were his words, confessing his own severity; "I will not equivocate; I will not excuse; I will not retreat a single inch; and I will be heard.". . .

Garrison soon found northern sympathizers, some of whom were ready to devote wealth and social influence to this new crusade; and among his earliest personal friends were Sewall and Ellis Gray Loring, of Boston, and the generous Tappan brothers, of New York. With the publication of the *Liberator*, the idea was put forth of organizing anti-slavery societies upon its aggressive platform; and Garrison looked to the abolitionists of England, whose work for the British colonies was greatly advanced by means of such associations. But here the practical obstacles were very great. Bible, tract, missionary, and temperance societies absorbed the zeal of thousands who were bent on doing good but dared not touch the plague-spot. Dr. Channing, New England's great leader of liberal thought, was a timid and critical observer, though slowly bracing himself to be outspoken as the friend of the slave; Webster wished for the constitution as it was, and the Union unimpaired; and Everett, as little of a soldier as ever breathed, offered to buckle on the knapsack, shoulder a musket, and march to the aid of his southern brethren, whenever their lives should be jeopardized by a slave uprising. Such influences dominated the vicinity. Not until the close of 1831 did the first of these new anti-slavery societies take initial steps, which led, early in the new year, to its organization on a dark and stormy night in the humble school-room of a colored Baptist church. Twelve persons, all white, subscribed their names and united as the "New England Anti-Slavery Society." A national association, known as the "American Anti-Slavery Society," was organized later. Ancillary societies sprang up rapidly at the North, though often dropping apart and recombining differently, since free-thinkers and disorganizers are not held easily to any plan of co-operation. None of their leaders, at all events, could command public opinion sufficiently to institute any real reform. But by lashing the Union into fury the abolitionists urged forward their cause; sleep was murdered when their harsh fire-bells startled the air. The early course of these societies showed indeed the radical difficulty they labored under of devising some plan, fair and feasible, for promoting their ends. They tended to anarchy, incendiarism, in all their actions; they sent not peace, but a sword. Garrison himself was a bomb-thrower, openly assaulting the constitution, because he saw it a strong prison-house. He tried in vain to induce freemen to abstain from buying slave-produced cotton and tobacco; instead of denouncing the crime of slavery, to identify the planter as a criminal, man-stealer, oppressor, pirate; to treat the constitution as a compact absolutely void for its guilt. None outside his small circle would embrace such tenets; to the constitution all true Americans clung as the ark of the covenant. But the new agitators were not long in sending a broadside into the American Colonization Society, now crippled with debt and seeking funds from the English abolitionists. Hastening abroad, as an emissary of the associations he had organized, Garrison, at the critical moment, assaulted that society so brilliantly on British soil as to destroy its prestige forever: the British philanthropists renounced its support, the great Wilberforce shortly before his death setting the example.

It was this same year that the great cause of emancipation in the British West Indies, to which Wilberforce, Clarkson, and their associates had so long directed their persevering efforts, triumphed in the passage of an act of Parliament. It provided a sort of preliminary apprentice system for the negroes, and compensation to their former owners. That statute which struck the fetters from eight hundred thousand colored people close to our Atlantic coast produced a profound impression upon our citizens, both South and North. In the glow of the moment, the Garrisonians, eager to infuse the British anti-slavery zeal into their own cause, committed a great indiscretion. They inflamed our sensitive community both by their unpatriotic comparisons, and by assuming to import foreign anti-slavery orators, as if to force the southern bulwark with the aid of the nation whose interference was of all foreign powers the most intolerable. Great Britain's abolition cause differed greatly from ours; hers was in a distant colony, ours at home; there insular opinion impressed a legislature competent to decree anything; and there, too, the freedom was not granted without terms considerate to the master, which our moralists scorned to imitate; for to recompense our slaveholder, so Garrison proclaimed, would be paying a thief for giving up stolen property and acknowledging his crime to be no crime.

The conflict thus violently opened did not cease in this Union until slavery was crushed by the heel of fratricidal war. The immediate fruit, at such a time, of inflammatory appeal on the one hand and slave insurrection on the other was mob outrage in northern cities, where the excitement most centred; and though, as in most mobs, the ignorant and vicious gained the upper hand, there was not wanting in these anti-slavery riots a sterling patriotism, which meant in its blind way to put down the wild anarchists, as they seemed to be, who were trying to subvert the pillars upon which rested the American fabric and the salvation of society. Bands of rowdies, during the turbulence of 1834 in Philadelphia and New York, broke up abolition meetings, attacked the presses, and threatened the persons of the chief agitators; they rampaged the negro quarters of the city, doing wanton mischief. But by 1835 the popular feeling against these "apostles of fanaticism" was exasperated by their own blind course of action. They had hired George Thompson, a British lecturer of imprudent speech, to harangue northern multitudes for immediate emancipation, a cause which northern States were powerless to effect peaceably. They had deluged the South with incendiary pamphlets, whose tendency, whether they so meant it or not, was to excite the slaves to rise against their masters. This latter appeal to terrorism was the device of the American Anti-Slavery Society, which set aside a large sum of money to circulate gratuitously their seditious writings where it was death to distribute them openly. Tracts and periodicals printed expressly for this purpose, with pictures even more inflammatory than the text they illustrated, —the master with scourge in his hand and his victim at his feet,—were struck off by the thousand, some printed on cheap muslin handkerchiefs, and deposited in the mails for the South. The best anti-slavery statesmen, such as Adams, have believed that the purpose was incendiary; and though agitators denied that they intended more than to reach the conscience of southern legislatures, this denial was not accepted; denying that they sent such documents to the slaves, they tacitly confessed mailing them to free blacks. The grave charge, never explicitly denied by them, that this was an experiment to terrify the master by kindling a new insurrection among the blacks, was made and reiterated by our whole people, and the abolitionists were deterred from trying such methods again. It was a foolish experiment; for, as white men handled the mails, the leather bags were sure to belch out this dangerous matter. A package of these tracts discovered at Philadelphia was taken to the middle of the Delaware river and sunk there. In Charleston the mail-pouches were emptied of such contents, and three thousand citizens gathered by night to see a bonfire made of the documents and the chief men of the anti-slavery societies hung and burned in effigy. A Richmond meeting invoked the interference of the Postmaster-General to stop the delivery of such infamous matter, and adjured all Union brethren at the North to repress the societies issuing them "by strong yet lawful means." The North was not mute in this emergency. Meetings in New York, and in most other large cities, were held to denounce all Southampton methods of emancipation. In Boston's Faneuil Hall Mayor Lyman presided at a meeting of respectable citizens, who were addressed by Seth Sprague and Harrison Gray Otis. Instead of purging himself of suspicion, Garrison, in his paper, turned tauntingly upon this meeting: the cradle of liberty, he said, has become the refuge of slavery. This incensed the citizens more than ever against him; and it so happened that George Thompson, his imported friend, now upon his inflammatory tour, said in one of his intemperate speeches that southern slaves ought, or at least had a right, to cut the throats of their masters. Boston was becoming too hot to hold these two men. While Garrison kept out of the city, a double gallows was set up for a warning before his house; and when, a few weeks later, the British disturber was announced by posters to address a women's anti-slavery meeting by day in the busiest quarter of the city, a crowd which quickly swelled from a hundred to five thousand persons gathered about the building, which stood on the east side of Washington street, a little below the old State House, at that time occupied as the City Hall. It was early in the afternoon. Thompson, the chief object of their rage, did not arrive; and, increasing in turbulence with their numbers, the mob forced the women's meeting to adjourn. Still besieging the entrance to this building, they next turned their thoughts to the editor of the *Liberator,* who was known to be inside. Garrison fled by the rear, but, being caught, was led unresistingly from the back yard through a crooked lane into State street, a rope about his body and his clothing partly torn. While his captors were irresolute what to do with him, many proposing that he should be ducked in the frog-pond, a few stalwart men in the crowd, who pitied his plight and were unwilling that their own fellow-citizen should take the punishment intended for an English brawler, managed to hustle Garrison into the City Hall opposite, where, on the advice of the mayor, whom his press had been abusing, he consented to be put into a close carriage and driven through the crowd to the jail, where he remained all night, as if under arrest, and was then released. Escaping further violence by this stratagem, he left Boston secretly the next day, self-exiled for a season, though issuing his newspaper from that city as before. Thompson, the lecturer, warned in good season by the angry aspect of his audiences, suddenly disappeared, cutting his tour short, and was smuggled out of the United States in a sailing-vessel.

Such were the early episodes which gave Garrison and his fellow-apostles a picturesque place in our annals, though the worst sufferers for the cause at present were the poor negroes their zeal had befriended. Subsiding now into smoother and more legitimate channels of influence, and dividing, moreover, among themselves upon the ways and means of agitation, they were soon favored by the current of events, though untractable theorists to the last. They were not actors in affairs, but agitators, critics, come-outers, coiners of cutting epithets, who scourged men in public station with as little mercy as ever the slave-driver did his victim, less pleased that their work was being done than displeased because it was not done faster. Their political blunders widened the chasm between North and South, and their constant instigation was to throttle that law which was the breath of our being, to trample down the Union rather than convert, constrain, or conquer slavery behind the shield of the constitution. This was because of their fanaticism. Not one leader of this school ever took a responsible part in affairs, or co-operated in lawful and practical measures for promoting the reform they caressed in their preaching. But whatever interpretation this crusade for immediate abolition might admit of, it could have no effect South, unless by terrifying the masters in the slave States, those robbers and man-stealers, who—strange paradox—were under the municipal law no robbers, no criminals at all. It did not terrify, but it hardened them; and wounded pride made them more determined than ever to maintain their system, come what might,—to rivet it more firmly upon the Union, or else to leave the Union and set up for themselves. In the North, however, the anti-slavery cause grew and continued to grow, for the agitators were felt to be in earnest and morally right. This early violence was regretted; it reacted favorably to abolition, and the abolitionists might scold and censure henceforth under the license of free discussion. The chief "apostle and martyr of emancipation," though ceasing not to irritate, was molested no more at home; and Boston, the seat of Whig sobriety, was spared those grosser scenes of riot and destruction which disgraced the Jacksonian cities in these turbulent years. The *Liberator* still forged its thunderbolts, and, though social disdain long pursued Garrison and his friends, embittered by the caustic severity of their pen and speech, their moral firmness gained sympathizers, as it always does: their one idea was abstractly right. The essential gain of all this was to awaken the northern conscience from its long sleep, and force up opinion to the healthier plane of conforming the human decree to the divine; as for the slave, the negro, he rose to be an object of sentiment, rarely seen, little comprehended, never studied on his plantation surroundings, and personal or race sympathy had nothing scarcely to do with raising up champions for him. Garrison had the spirit of prophecy, nor was he wholly mistaken when, on taking up his parable, he wrote, "Posterity will bear testimony that I was right." Better this agitation, though it sent a two-edged sword, than the poisonous lethargy before it; better a quarter-century of sharp collision, followed by the desperate struggle for the mastery, than another century of corrupt growth and bonded misalliance. Hate-producing as were the winged words of these agitators, no gentler purgative, perhaps, could have done the work; for in all moral reforms, as philosophy teaches us, and wherever God's image becomes distorted in the mirror of human custom, change works in a progressive cycle: fearless reproof brings persecution of the reprover, persecution brings sympathy, sympathy leads to reaction, and reaction to reformation. But too complex were the agencies which now began working out the slave's salvation for any one man or set of men to appropriate them. Whether one shall admire most the bold denunciator, whose speech irritates thought into action, or the enlightened statesman, who accomplishes for reform all that his age will admit and respects the limitations of social ordinance, or the grim warrior who wins the fight, his temperament must decide. History should do justice to all; and, though timid and truckling at times, that public conscience is not to be despised which long struggled between moral obligation and loyalty until loyalty itself opened the means of escaping the curse.

21

James Ford Rhodes (1892)[1]

Of the historians in the postwar generation, the one who wrote in the most authoritative and acceptable way on the Civil War era was James Ford Rhodes, an Ohioan. Rhodes's compromise version of the struggle—which satisfied many in both sections—maintained that the North had been right to attack slavery but wrong to impose Negro suffrage upon the South during Reconstruction. His account of Garrison is an illustration of his general thesis about the moral superiority of the North on the slavery issue. Unlike Wilson, he does not describe Garrison as having been too extreme to have much direct influence in the North. Rather, he plays down Garrison's radicalism and portrays him and his followers as having laid the foundation for the Republican Party by arousing the Northern conscience.

In August of this year (1831) occurred the Nat Turner insurrection in Virginia, which seemed to many Southerners a legitimate fruit of the bold teaching of Garrison, although there was indeed between the two events no real connection. But this negro rising struck terror through the South and destroyed calm reason. The leader, Nat Turner, a genuine African of exceptional capacity, knowing the Bible by heart, prayed and preached to his fellow-slaves. He told them of the voices he heard in the air, of the visions he saw, and of his communion with the Holy Spirit. An eclipse of the sun was a sign that they must rise and slay their enemies who had deprived them of freedom. The massacre began at night and continued for forty-eight hours; women and children were not spared, and before the bloody work was checked sixty-one whites were victims of negro ferocity. The retribution was terrible. Negroes were shot, hanged, tortured, and burned to death, and all on whom suspicion lighted met a cruel fate. In Southampton County, the

[1] From James Ford Rhodes, *History of the United States from the Compromise of 1850* (New York, 1892), I, 56–63.

scene of the insurrection, there was a reign of terror, and alarm spread throughout the slave States.

This event, and the thought that it might be the precursor of others of the same kind, account for much of the Southern rage directed against Garrison and his crusade. Nor, when we reflect on the sparsely settled country, the wide distance between plantations—conditions that made a negro insurrection possible—and when we consider what it was for planters to have hanging over their heads the horrors of a servile war, will it seem surprising that judicial poise of temper was impossible when Southerners discussed the work of Garrison. They regarded it as an incitement for their slaves to revolt. But they did injustice to Garrison, for Nat Turner had never seen a copy of the *Liberator,* and the paper had not a single subscriber south of the Potomac. Nor did Garrison ever send a pamphlet or paper to any slave, nor advocate the right of physical resistance on the part of the oppressed. He was a non-resistant, and did not believe that force should be used to overturn legal authority, even when unjustly and oppressively exercised. The assertion that slavery is a damning crime is one thing; the actual incitement of slaves to insurrection is another. The distinction between the two was not appreciated at the South. Stringent laws were made against the circulation of the *Liberator,* and vigilance committees sent their warnings to any who were supposed to have a part in spreading its doctrines. In North Carolina Garrison was indicted for a felony, and the legislature of Georgia offered a reward of five thousand dollars for the arrest and conviction of the editor or publisher. One voice went abroad from public officials, popular meetings, and from the press of the South, demanding that the governor of Massachusetts or the mayor of Boston should suppress the "infernal *Liberator.*"

The people of Virginia had often struggled to free themselves from the coils of slavery, and the Nat Turner insurrection furnished the occasion for another attempt. At the following session of the Legislature a proposition was made to inquire into the expediency of some plan of gradual emancipation. In the debate that took place on the subject, the evil of slavery was characterized in terms as strong as an abolitionist could have used. The alarm excited all over the South by the negro rising in Southampton County was not, one member explained, from the fear of Nat Turner, but it was on account of "the suspicion eternally attached to the slave himself—a suspicion that a Nat Turner might be in every family, that the same bloody deed might be acted over at any time, and in any place; that the materials for it were spread through the land, and were always ready for a like explosion."

But a majority of the House of Representatives, in which the project was discussed, could not be had for ordering an inquiry, and the further consideration of the subject was indefinitely postponed. It has sometimes been asserted that had not the abolitionist agitation begun, this Virginia movement would have resulted in the gradual emancipation of slaves in that state; but there is, in truth, no reason for thinking that anything more would have come of it than from previous abortive attempts in the same direction. On many pages of Virginia history may one read of noble efforts by noble men towards freeing their State from slavery. But the story of the end is a repeated tale; the seeds sown fell among thorns, and the thorns sprung up and choked them.

Meanwhile Garrison and his little band continued the uphill work of proselyting at the North, and especially in Boston. Merchants, manufacturers, and capitalists were against the movement, for trade with the South was important, and they regarded the propagation of abolition sentiments as injurious to the commercial interests of Boston. Good society turned the back upon the abolitionists. Garrison had no college education to recommend him to an aristocracy based partly upon wealth and partly upon culture. The churches were bitterly opposed to the movement. Oliver Johnson, one of the early disciples of Garrison, relates that several times his efforts were in vain to persuade some one among a dozen white clergymen of Boston to open an anti-slavery meeting with prayer, and he was in each case forced at last to accept the services of a negro preacher from "Negro Hill." The position of the church was well expressed by a noted clergyman, who attributed the sin of slavery to a past generation, and assigned the duty of emancipation to future generations. The abolitionists, however, gradually gained ground. The year 1833 was for them one of grateful memory. Then, at Philadelphia, the American Anti-slavery Society was organized by delegates who made up in enthusiasm what they lacked in numbers. The Declaration of Sentiments, drawn up by Garrison, was a paper worthy of the earnest and intelligent people who were its signers. It referred to the immortal Declaration adopted in the same city fifty-seven years before, and, as the strongest abolition argument that could be made, quoted the phrase "that all men are created equal; that they are endowed by their Creator with certain inalienable rights;

that among these are life, liberty, and the pursuit of happiness." It denounced slavery in vigorous terms, yet conceded that Congress had no right to interfere with it in the States; and while condemning the employment of material force in any way to promote abolition, the signers pledged themselves to use moral means, so far as lay in their power, to overthrow the execrable system of slavery. This was not an inflammatory and seditious appeal; the delegates were men of good character, pure morals, and were law-abiding citizens; yet it was necessary for the police to guard the convention hall against threatened mob violence. The meeting was regarded by all Southern people, and by nearly all at the North, in much the same way as we should now look upon an assemblage of anarchists. . . .

Excitement about the abolition movement characterized the year 1835. Numerous public meetings and the press of the South demanded almost with one voice that the abolitionists must be put down or they would destroy the Union. A suspension of commercial intercourse with the North was even suggested. The Charleston post-office was forcibly entered and a large number of tracts and papers sent there by the American Anti-slavery Society were seized; the next night these papers and effigies of Garrison and other abolitionists were burned in the presence of a large number of spectators. On a false alarm of a projected slave rising in Mississippi, several white men and negroes were hanged by vigilance committees. The wrath of the Southern people against the abolitionists was reflected at the North, and the feeling grew that the imputation of abolition ideas to the whole Northern community must be repelled. As the *Liberator* could not be suppressed, nor anti-slavery meetings prohibited by law, recourse was had to mob violence. Attacks upon abolitionists had previously been common, and this sort of warfare culminated in the year 1835. A ferocious anti-negro riot took place at Philadelphia. Rev. Samuel May, a devoted abolitionist and adherent of Garrison, was mobbed at Haverhill, Mass., the home of Whittier, and five times afterwards at different places in Vermont. A disgraceful anti-slavery riot occurred at Utica, N. Y. In Boston, on the same day, a mob, variously estimated at from two thousand to five thousand, including many gentlemen of property and influence, broke up a meeting of the Boston Female Anti-slavery Society. Garrison, one of the men against whom the mob directed its fury, had escaped from the hall in which the ladies were assembled, but he was seized and dragged bareheaded through the streets, subjected to indignity and insult, and his life was threatened. The mayor and police finally rescued him from the hands of the rioters, and put him in jail as a protection against further violence.

Yet the work of converting and creating Northern sentiment went on. In spite of misrepresentation, obloquy, and derision, the abolitionists continued to apply moral ideas and Christian principles to the institution of slavery. The teachings of Christ and the Apostles actuated this crusade, and its latent power was great. If one looks for its results merely to the numbers of congressmen chosen by the abolitionists, to the vote received by presidential candidates distinctively theirs, or even to the number of members enrolled in the anti-slavery societies, only a faint idea of the force of the movement will be gained. The influence of the *Liberator* cannot be measured by its subscribers, any more than the French revolutionists of 1789 can be reckoned as of no greater number than the readers of "The Social Contract." If Rousseau had never lived, said Napoleon, there would have been no French Revolution. It would be historical dogmatism to say that if Garrison had not lived, the Republicans would not have succeeded in 1860. But if we wish to estimate correctly the influence of Garrison and his disciples, we must not stop with the enumeration of their avowed adherents. We must bear in mind the impelling power of their positive dogmas, and of their never-ceasing inculcation on those who were already voters and on thinking youths who were to become voters, and who, in their turn, prevailed upon others. We must picture to ourselves this process of argument, of discussion, of persuasion, going on for twenty-five years, with an ever-increasing momentum, and we cannot resist the conviction that this anti-slavery agitation had its part, and a great part too, in the first election of Lincoln. It was due to Garrison and his associates that slavery became a topic of discussion at every Northern fireside. Those who had heard the new doctrine gladly tried to convince their family and their friends; those who were but half convinced wished to vanquish their doubts or have put to rest the rising suspicion that they were partners in a great wrong; those who stubbornly refused to listen could not fail to feel that a new force had made its appearance, with which a reckoning must be made. Slavery could not bear examination. To describe it was to condemn it. There was a certain fitness, therefore, in the demand of the Southerners that the discussion of slavery in any shape should be no longer permitted at the North.

But in what a state of turpitude the North would have been if it had not bred abolitionists! If the abolitionists had not prepared the way, how would the political rising of 1854–60 against the slave power have been possible? It is true that many ardent Republicans who voted for Lincoln would have repudiated the notion that they were in any way influenced by the arguments of Garrison and his associates. And it is equally true that in 1835 the average Northern man satisfied himself by thinking slavery in the abstract a great evil, but that, as it existed in the South, it was none of his concern; he thought that "God hath made of one blood all nations of men" a good doctrine to be preached on Sunday, and "all men are created equal" a fit principle to be proclaimed on the Fourth of July; but he did not believe that these sentiments should be applied to the social condition of the South. But that was exactly the ground on which the abolitionists planted themselves, and, by stirring the national conscience, they made possible the formation of a political party whose cardinal principle was opposition to the extension of slavery, and whose reason for existence lay in the belief of its adherents that slavery in the South was wrong.

22

John Jay Chapman (1913)[1]

John Jay Chapman's view of Garrison was unlike that of either Schouler or Rhodes. Where Schouler was critical of Garrison, Chapman was adulatory. If Rhodes tried to domesticate Garrison's radicalism and adapt it to the framework of late nineteenth-century liberalism, Chapman recognized Garrison's anarchistic bent and approved of it. An essayist and cultural critic with independent and original views, Chapman was a latter-day abolitionist in his attitude toward the race problem. His thinking was so unorthodox for his time that his interpretation of Garrison made little impression on his contemporaries and clearly falls outside the mainstream of antislavery historiography. But his work does constitute a kind of link between the abolitionists themselves and the neo-abolitionists of a later period. The following excerpt from his biography is perhaps the most eloquent defense of Garrison ever penned. Like his subject, Chapman does not "excuse," "equivocate," or "retreat a single inch."

Garrison was a man of action, that is to say, a man to whom ideas were revealed in relation to passing events, and who saw in ideas the levers and weapons with which he might act upon the world. A seer on the other hand is a man who views passing events by the light of ideas, and who counts upon his vision, not upon his action, for influence. The seer feels that the mere utterance of his thought, nay the mere vision of it, fulfills his function. Garrison was not a man of this kind. His mission was more lowly, more popular, more visible; and his intellectual grasp was restricted and uncertain. Garrison was a man of the market-place. Language to him was not the mere means of stating truth, but a mace to break open a jail. He was to be the instrument of great and rapid changes in public opinion during an epoch of terrible and fluctuating excitement. The thing which he is

---

[1] From John Jay Chapman, *William Lloyd Garrison* (Boston, 1921), pp. 162–76. (Originally published in 1913.)

to see, to say, and to proclaim, from moment to moment, is as freshly given to him by prodigal nature, is as truly spontaneous, as the song of the thrush. He never calculates, he acts upon inspiration; he is always ingenuous, innocent, self-poised, and, as it were, inside of some self-acting machinery which controls his course, and rolls out the carpet of his life for him to walk on. We must remember this; for it is almost impossible not to use words which imply the contrary in describing the acts of the practical man—the man who utters sharp sayings in order to gain attention, the man who gives no quarter when in the ring.

In reviewing the life of such a man we must take the logic of it as a whole; we must feel the unity of it as an organic process and torrent of force. It will contain many breaks in metaphysical unity; yet through these breaks may be seen the gushing stream of the spirit. I believe that Garrison shifted his ground and changed his mind less often than most men of that kaleidoscopic epoch. But we must not try to make him out more consistent than he was. All politics, including reform agitation, proceeds from day to day and from year to year under the illusion that the thing in hand is more important than it really is. All the actors are at every moment somewhat deceived; and to each of them the thing in hand ever a little blots out the sky. The agitator lives in a realm of exaggeration, of broadsides and italic types, of stampings of the foot and clenchings of the hand. He uses the terms and phrases of immortal truth to clamp together his leaky raft. The "belle réponse" of the martyr, the deep apothegm of the sage, and the words of Christ, are ever on his lips. Such things pass muster in politics without exciting comment. And yet, these statements of ideal truth, like the axioms of arithmetic, never quite square with the material world. They can only be felt and believed in mentally. You can never find or measure out an exact pound of anything or lay off a true mile; nor can you assign any accurate value to the influence of a good deed. Nevertheless, the inaccuracy which is permissible in the marketplace is very much greater than the inaccuracy permissible to the historian who sits in his closet endeavoring to think clearly upon the matter.

The source of Garrison's power was the Bible. From his earliest days he read the Bible constantly, and prayed constantly. It was with this fire that he started his conflagration. Now the Bible is many things. It is a key to metaphysical truth, it is a compendium of large human wisdom, it is a code of ethics, it is the history of a race, and many other things beside. To Garrison, the Bible was the many-piped organ to which he sang the song of his life, and the arsenal from which he drew the weapons of his warfare. I doubt if any man ever knew the Bible so well, or could produce a text to fit a political emergency with such startling felicity as Garrison. Take for example, the text provided by him for Wendell Phillips's speech on the Sunday morning following Lincoln's call for troops in 1861. "Therefore thus saith the Lord; Ye have not hearkened unto me in proclaiming liberty everyone to his brother, and every man to his neighbor: behold, I proclaim a liberty for you, saith the Lord, to the sword, to the pestilence, and to the famine."

I doubt whether Cromwell or Milton could have rivaled Garrison in this field of quotation; and the power of quotation is as dreadful a weapon as any which the human intellect can forge. From his boyhood upward Garrison's mind was soaked in the Bible and in no other book. His "Causes" are all drawn from the Bible, and most of them may be traced to the phrases and thoughts of Christ, as for instance Peace (Peace I give unto you), Perfectionism (Be ye therefore perfect), Non-resistance (Resist not evil), Anti-sabbatarianism (The Lord is Lord of the Sabbath). So also, a prejudice against all fixed forms of worship, against the authority of human government, against every binding of the spirit into conformity with human law—all these things grew up in Garrison's mind out of his Bible readings; as they have done in the minds of so many other men before and after him. He, himself, was not going to be bound, and never was bound, by any declaration nor by any document. He even arrived at distrusting the Bible itself, perceiving that the Bible itself was often a tyrant— much as Christ saw the tyranny of the law of Moses. All this part of Garrison's mental activity is his true vocation. Here he rages like a lion of Judah. By these onslaughts he is freeing people from their mental bonds: he is shaking down the palaces of Babylon.

His age was the age of social experiments, and he was ever ready to take on a new one. This hospitality to new dogmas annoyed his associates, and led, as we have seen, to revolts, schisms, and heresies in the Anti-slavery ranks. Garrison seems to have been assailed by such multitudinous revelations from on high that he was obliged to publish one dispensation in order to clear the wires for the next. There is one of these manifestoes which reveals the impromptu character of them all. "Despite its length," says the biographers, "the greater part of this important document must be given here." There follow several pages of fine print, concerning the causes uppermost in Garrison's mind, which evidently had filled up all the space in the *Liberator,* or used up all the ink in the office; and yet it appears at the close, that Garrison has forgotten to say anything about woman's rights. And so he calls out, like a man upon a departing stage-coach: "As our object is *universal emancipation,* to redeem women as well as men from a servile to an equal condition—we shall go for the RIGHTS OF WOMEN to their utmost extent."

In those days societies were founded for everything. No one ever paused to consider what things could or could not be accomplished through organization, nor how far the sayings of Christ were parts of one another, nor whether at the bottom of all these questions there lay some truth which enveloped them all. Every one rushed to utterance, and Garrison more than all men put together. So long as we consider his utterances in the large, as part of the upturning of that age, as the *sine qua non* of a new epoch, we love and value them. It is only when we collocate them, analyze them, and try to find something for our own souls in them, that they turn out to be emergency cries. They were designed towards local ends, they were practical politics, they do not always cohere with one another.

The great thesis to which he devoted his life, however, was unquestionably sound. He thus announced it in the *Liberator* in 1832:

> There is much declamation about the sacredness of the compact which was formed between the free and slave States, on the adoption of the Constitution. A sacred compact, forsooth! We pronounce it the most bloody and heaven-daring arrangement ever made by men for the continuance and protection of a system of the most atrocious villainy ever exhibited upon the earth. Yes, we recognize the compact, but with feelings of shame and indignation; and it will be held in everlasting infamy by the friends of justice and humanity throughout the world. It was a compact formed at the sacrifice of the bodies and souls of millions of our race, for the sake of achieving a political object—an unblushing and monstrous coalition to do evil that good might come. Such a compact was in the nature of things, and according to the law of God, null and void from the beginning. No body of men ever had the right to guarantee the holding of human beings in bondage.
>
> Who or what were the framers of our Government that they should dare confirm and authorize such high-handed villainy—such a flagrant robbery of the inalienable rights of man—such a glaring violation of all the precepts and injunctions of the Gospel—such a savage war upon a sixth part of our whole population? They were men, like our-

selves—as fallible, as sinful, as weak, as ourselves. By the infamous bargain which they made between themselves, they virtually dethroned the Most High God, and trampled beneath their feet their own solemn and heaven-attested Declaration, that all men are created equal, and endowed by their Creator with certain inalienable rights—among which are life, liberty, and the pursuit of happiness. They had no lawful power to bind themselves or their posterity for one hour—for one moment—by such an unholy alliance. It was not valid then—it is not valid now. Still they persisted in maintaining it—and still do their successors, the people of Massachusetts, of New England, and of the twelve free States, persist in maintaining it. A sacred compact! a sacred compact! What, then, is wicked and ignominious?

It is said that if you agitate this question you will divide the Union. Believe it not; but should disunion follow, the fault will not be yours. You must perform your duty, faithfully, fearlessly and promptly, and leave the consequences to God: that duty clearly is, to cease from giving countenance and protection to Southern kidnappers. Let them separate, if they can muster courage enough—and the liberation of their slaves is certain. Be assured that slavery will very speedily destroy this Union *if it be let alone;* but even if the Union can be preserved by treading upon the necks, spilling the blood, and destroying the souls of millions of your race, we say it is not worth a price like this, and that it is in the highest degree criminal for you to continue the present compact. Let the pillars thereof fall—let the superstructure crumble into dust— if it must be upheld by robbery and oppression.

This statement of Garrison's is, to my mind, the best thing ever said about slavery in the United States. There is no exaggeration in the statement: it is absolutely true. It is a complete answer to the Constitutional point; and makes all our ante-bellum public men (including Lincoln) appear a little benighted. They are like men who have been born in a darkness and have lived always in a twilight. They all have a slight, congenital weakness of the eye, which prevents them from taking the daylight view of this whole matter.

We ourselves to-day are so habituated to the historic obfuscation of our ancestors that we make allowance for it—more allowance, indeed, than we ought to make. We have, by inheritance, rather weak eyes on this subject ourselves. The true cause for wonder as to the age of Abolition is not that Garrison was right, but that there should have been only one person in America with a clear head. Let us now turn forward over ten years of history—including all the pictures of struggle and incidents referred to in the earlier pages, and let us read Garrison's most famous exposition of his theme uttered in 1842:

> We affirm that the Union is not of heaven. It is founded in unrighteousness and cemented with blood. It is the work of men's hands, and they worship the idol which they have made. It is a horrible mockery of freedom. In all its parts and proportions it is misshapen, incongruous, unnatural. The message of the prophet to the people in Jerusalem describes the exact character of our "republican" Compact: "Hear the Word of the Lord, ye scornful men that rule this people. Because ye have said, We have made a covenant with Death, and with Hell are we at agreement; when the overflowing scourge shall pass through, it shall not come unto us: for we have made lies our refuge, and under falsehood have we hid ourselves: Therefore thus saith the Lord God, Judgment will I lay to the line, and righteousness to the plummet: and the hail shall sweep away the refuge of lies, and the water shall overflow the hiding-place. And your covenant with Death *shall be annulled,* and your agreement with Hell *shall not stand;* when the overflowing scourge shall pass through then ye shall be trodden down by it."
>
> Another message of the same inspired prophet is equally applicable: "Thus saith the Holy One of Israel, Because ye despised this word, and trust in oppression and perverseness, and stay thereon: Therefore, this iniquity shall be to you *as a breach ready to fall,* swelling out in a high wall, whose breaking cometh suddenly, AT AN INSTANT. And he shall break it as the breaking of a potter's vessel that is broken to pieces; he shall not spare: so that there shall not be found in the bursting of it, a sherd to take fire from the hearth, or to take water withal out of the pit."
>
> Slavery is a combination of Death and Hell, and with it the North have made a covenant and are at agreement. As an element of the Government it is omnipotent, omniscient, omnipresent. As a component part of the Union it is necessarily a national interest. Divorced from Northern protection it dies; with that protection, it enlarges its boundaries, multiplies its victims, and extends its ravages.

These passages are too direct to be called extravagant. They are appalling. They are magnificent. And they came much nearer to expressing the general opinion of the country in 1842 than the milder words quoted above came to expressing the contemporary opinion of 1832. Education was marching, the case was beginning to be understood. Within three years after Garrison's denunciation of the Constitution as an agreement with Hell, the Annexation of Texas brought thousands of the most conservative minds in the country, including Channing, to the point of abandoning the Constitution; and when in 1854 Garrison publicly burned the Constitution on the Fourth of July, the incident was of slight importance. Civil War was already inevitable: the dragon's teeth had been sown: the blades of bright bayonets could be seen pushing up through the soil in Kansas.

We see, then, the profound unity of Garrison's whole course, and may examine with indulgence some minor failures in logic which are very characteristic of him—very characteristic, indeed, of all practical-minded men who, after making one fault of logic, proceed to joggle themselves back again to their true work by committing a second. It is apparent that a man who assumes Garrison's grounds as to the importance of the spirit, and the unimportance of everything else, can never turn aside and adopt any institution, without doing violence to his own principles. To disparage all government because it is "the letter that killeth," and thereafter to swear fealty to some party, or adopt a symbol, or advise a friend to vote with the Whigs is inconsistent. One who believes in standing for *absolute* principle can never indorse some political scheme on the ground that "this time it doesn't count." One who believes it wrong to meet force with force cannot retain the privilege of approving some particular war or some particular act of self-defense, which seems to him to be useful. Garrison had not the mental training to perceive this, and to do so would have involved his retirement from the camp to the closet: it would have involved his being someone else. Suffice it to say that from time to time his nature drew a veil over his theories, and so obscured them that he was able to support the Constitution of the United States, to rejoice in bloodshed, to take active part in political contests,—both in the great occasional National elections (as when he came out for Lincoln or Frémont), and in the continuous petty politics of the Anti-slavery cause.

After having supported one of these human institutions with zeal, and having justified his conduct with facile and self-deceiving casuistry, he would again ascend the mountain, the veil would be withdrawn from his intellect, and he would see his true vision once more and proclaim it with renewed fervor: the vision, namely, that no institution should be held sacred.

23
Gilbert Hobbs Barnes (1933)[1]

From an historiographic point of view, Gilbert Hobbs Barnes's The Antislavery Impulse *(1933) is probably the most important study of the abolitionist movement ever published. Barnes rescued from oblivion the Western abolitionists—Theodore Weld, James G. Birney, and their followers—and made a case for their primacy in the movement. To establish his point, Barnes contended that Garrison, previously regarded as the central figure in the antislavery enterprise, was at best useless to the movement and at worst a serious impediment to its success. Barnes's basic attitude toward the abolitionists in general has been a matter of controversy. His vigorous attack upon Garrison and some of his comments about the broader movements show the influence of the "revisionist" interpretation of the Civil War—a view that was coming into prominence in the 1930's. Its thesis was that the war had been the needless result of fanaticism and hysteria. At the same time, however, Barnes's treatment of the motivation of Weld and his associates went against the revisionist current by taking seriously the religious and moral basis of the abolitionist movement. By virtue of this latter emphasis, Barnes can be seen as a forerunner of the later "neo-abolitionist" school of antislavery historiography.*

The selections that follow all place Garrison in a highly unfavorable light and demonstrate what has been until very recently, the dominant modern image of him. The first section describes Garrison at the founding convention of the American Anti-Slavery Society, the second and third constitute a discussion of Garrison's quarrel with the New England clergy, and the fourth and fifth deal with Garrison's takeover of the American Anti-Slavery Society and its aftermath.

[1] From Gilbert Hobbs Barnes, *The Antislavery Impulse, 1830–1844* (New York, 1933), pp. 55–58, 91–94, 97–99, 169–70, 174 f. Copyright © 1933 by the American Historical Association; copyright renewed 1961 by Elizabeth Barnes Pumphrey. Reprinted by permission of Elizabeth Barnes Pumphrey.

As national conventions went in the benevolent empire, the meeting was a convention only in name. The shortness of the notice, the unseasonable time of the year, and the muddy winter roads had prevented all but a handful of reformers from attending. Few of them represented societies; the greater number were correspondents of Arthur Tappan. Some, like George Bourne, were ardent abolitionists of the old school. A few of the Pennsylvania society came—Atlee, Coates, and Lewis—and Negro delegates were there in some force. Theodore Weld, an abstainer from conventions "on principle," would not come; but he wrote from Lane Seminary pledging his efforts and prayers to the cause, and he was elected to the board of managers of the society. In all there were only sixty in attendance—a committee rather than a convention of delegates. As a representative gathering to establish an antislavery movement throughout the nation, it was a fiasco.

But for Garrison personally the meeting was one of the great occasions of his life. With the glory of his British ordination still about him, he seemed to the delegates—pledged as they were to the British precedent—like a Moses from Sinai, bearing the tablets of the law to his people. His face still shone with the reflected glory of his triumph overseas. He had breakfasted with Buxton; he had communed with Henry Brougham; Wilberforce himself had summoned him and blessed his labors in America. The delegates saw in him their ordained priest, the vicegerent of the British movement in America. Speeches were devoted to his praise. Resolutions were passed in his honor. "He has won the confidence of the people of England," said Lewis Tappan. "We ought to put that honored name in the forefront of our ranks." They did so. As Leonard Bacon, leading clergyman of Connecticut, scornfully remarked, Garrison was "the man whom they assembled a national convention to glorify."

He retired from the session and wrote a Declaration of Sentiments to which the convention listened with reverent attention and adopted with hardly a change. It was the first time in the new movement that an anti-slavery society had uttered a declaration without claiming the British precedent; for Garrison, always ready to think well of himself, had accepted the investiture of the British precedent, and he felt no need to refer to its greatness to enhance his own.

Here began the Garrison legend—consolidated by later events—that he was the leader of the anti-slavery movement in America. The members of the convention left Philadelphia pledged to maintain the legend against all detractors; and they did their work so well that for a time abolitionists everywhere not only accepted the popular identification of the national movement with Garrison and his works, but acclaimed it as a truth!

His reputation thus established, Garrison cashed it in. At a meeting of the executive committee of the new society immediately after the adjournment of the convention, "called," said Garrison, "for the purpose of hearing my statements respecting the embarrassments of the Liberator, I stated that . . . relief should at once be given to the Liberator; otherwise the paper must inevitably go down. I remember that all who were present expressed deep sympathy," but nobody offered anything more substantial. However, Garrison had a scheme: "I stated that Mr. Knapp and myself had on hand about $1,000 worth of anti-slavery publications . . . which, inasmuch as we could not dispose of them, were a dead weight sinking us to earth." He proposed that the society purchase enough of these unsalable pamphlets to relieve the *Liberator*; "but several of the committee raised some *constitutional* or rather financial objections to the purchasing of the publications alluded to, inasmuch as the Parent Society was then destitute of funds. . . . At last, on motion, it was voted that the Society purchase of Garrison & Knapp, publications to the amount of $440—to be paid for as soon as possible." With unspeakable relief, Garrison then turned to Arthur Tappan and told him "that it would not be necessary to raise the whole sum of $440, inasmuch as I owed Rev. Mr. Paul, then in England, $200 . . . and which I desired and was requested by Mr. Paul to pay immediately into the hands of Arthur Tappan." The Society could now owe Arthur Tappan the two hundred dollars, he informed the perplexed president; Tappan in turn could owe it to Paul, and he himself was thus cleared of all indebtedness. The remaining two hundred and forty dollars of the society's pledge, Lewis Tappan generously advanced to Garrison out of his own pocket. "This arrangement," Garrison declared, "saved the life of the Liberator."

Though Garrison's elevation in the new society enabled him to discharge his debt to Nathaniel Paul (at least so far as his conscience was concerned), and to save the *Liberator,* it did no sort of benefit to the cause. Indeed, it was a disaster second only to the endorsement of immediate emancipation; for his notoriety fixed upon the society a "vague and indefinite odium" which hampered its growth from the beginning. Moreover the manner of his exaltation began in the anti-slavery movement a disposition to glorify men instead of measures, which Weld acutely called one of "the greatest perils of the anti-slavery cause." Such eulogies as those to Garrison, Weld prophesied, were bound in time to stir "one of the basest sediments at the bottom of Human Depravity." Such fulsome honors to "the individual instead of the cause" would inevitably provoke rivalries for priority between the "idolatrized leaders," and rivalries such as these were sure to cause factional strife. " 'He that flattereth his neighbor spreadeth a net for his feet.' We abolitionists have dreadfully entangled our own and each other's feet. Murderous friendship!"

For all his elevation, Garrison never justified his priority by leadership. Indeed, he had no qualifications for leadership. His one office in the society, secretary of foreign correspondence, was soon resigned; and so long as the national organization held together he was never asked to fill another. He was so little a leader that even in the New England Anti-Slavery Society his journal was endured as its official organ for but a brief unhappy period. He was equipped by taste and temperament for free-lance journalism and for nothing else. As a journalist he was brilliant and provocative; as a leader for the anti-slavery host he was a name, an embodied motto, a figurehead of fanaticism.

*   *   *

In 1836, most abolitionists still considered Boston "the most important part of the field." For Bostonians believed that in projects of moral reform "Boston rules Massachusetts, Massachusetts rules New England and New England rules the nation"; and nowhere was this conviction deeper than among the abolitionists. Of them all, Garrison had the surest faith in Boston's moral primacy, especially in the anti-slavery cause; but in point of fact Boston abolitionism was in a bad way.

In sharp contrast to the Lane rebels, who first encountered hostility and then secured a hearing, Garrison first secured his hearing and then encountered hostility. In issue after issue of the *Liberator*, "his rancorous denunciations and his brawling, ferocious abuse" raised new opponents and embarrassed faithful friends. Upon the latter fell the burden of excusing his violence and propitiating his victims, a task which Garrison made more onerous by his growing tendency to advocate incidental causes along with immediatism. But these vagaries of his reforming spirit were minor irritants; the head of his offending was his promiscuous vilification of all individuals, institutions, and beliefs with which at the moment he did not agree.

From the beginning of the agitation, Garrison's "proneness to denunciation" had impeded the efforts of Boston abolitionists to extend the bounds of their society. "His spirit," they found, "affects too much . . . the reputation of the society," not only among prospective converts but also in the minds of clergymen to whom agents of "Garrisonism" applied for the use of their pulpits. There were objections and refusals; and leaders of the movement belatedly realized that their "chief task" was "to labor . . . for the purification of the New England churches," if their agents were to get a hearing. This meant that they must abolitionize the Congregational churches; for the Methodists insisted upon "doing their work in their own peculiar manner" through societies of their own, the Baptists were too decentralized to canvass as a church, and other creeds were inconsiderable.

In 1834, Amos A. Phelps, spokesman for the Boston society, appeared before the Association of the Congregational clergymen of Massachusetts and eloquently presented the claims of immediatism. He was too late. Two years before, Lyman Beecher had convinced the Congregational churches of New England that "union, blessed union" between colonizationists and abolitionists was desirable; and the association would concede to Phelps only "that the principles and objects of the American Anti-Slavery Society, so far as they do not come into collision with those of the American Colonization Society, meet with our approval."

However unsatisfactory this statement was to orthodox abolitionists, it implied a not unfriendly attitude and opened the way for further discussion. The discussion, however, was continued by Garrison, who described the statement as a cowardly and time-serving attempt to avoid a positive pronouncement and accused the Association of a "pro-slavery subservience" to the wishes of slaveholders. Further attempts to win the Congregational churches consequently encountered a less friendly attitude, and thenceforth they lived in the outer darkness of Garrison's disapproval.

Beecher's plan of union continued to exercise the Congregational clergy, and a year later, in 1835, it was embodied in formal organization, the ill-starred American Union for the Relief and Improvement of the Colored Race, which so bravely attempted a dispassionate and unbiassed survey of the Negro race in freedom and in slavery. It came to nothing, but for the time it disabled Congregational opposition to the abolitionists, pledged as it was to a peaceful union of all opinions to free the slave. Its failure, however, added bitterness to the growing hostility toward Garrison.

Meanwhile (1835–1836) in central New England, resistance to the Boston agitation increased. Agents were put in the field, itineraries were arranged, and meetings were well advertised; but more and more Congregational ministers denied their churches to "Garrisonism," often thereby closing their communities to the anti-slavery word. The agents protested; abolitionist minorities in the churches made trouble; and the *Liberator* dredged the language for epithets to characterize the offending clergymen. Such tactics did not open more churches; it increased rather than diminished the friction. One act of war led to another, and by the beginning of 1836 the heated editor of the *Liberator* was insisting that churches must open their pulpits to anti-slavery agitation, whatever their beliefs. If they expressed their unwillingness to do so, then "the wishes of pastor and churches are to be disregarded."

Before the controversy began, Garrison's religious views had been what Benjamin Lundy termed "ultra-orthodox"; but as his rancor toward the churches rose, his reverence for their claims declined. To justify his changing views he borrowed some of the heresies rife in the 'thirties, weaving them with self-righteous logic into his indictment of the churches. In an editorial upon Lyman Beecher's famous sermon in praise of the Sabbath, Garrison contended that the Sabbath was an outworn superstition. As various denominations failed to measure up to his standard of anti-slavery action, one by one they roused his ire. The Methodist church was "a cage of unclean birds and a synagogue of Satan"; the Presbyterian church was anathema; the Congregational ministers stood "at the head of the most implacable foes of God and man," toward whom "the most intense abhorrence should fill the breast of every disciple of Christ." Finally, when every creed had been denounced, he concluded that ecclesiastical institutions themselves confined the soaring spirit.

Once he had tasted the heady wine of anarchism, Garrison drank deep. Not only churches but other institutions as well were useless. By 1836, Garrison had "renounced all allegiance to his country and had nominated Jesus Christ to the Presidency of the United States and the World." His new beliefs he advocated with vigor and eloquence in the columns of the *Liberator*.

His novel heresies completed Garrison's alienation from orthodoxy. Methodists and Baptists, most orthodox of denominations, could not be expected to connive at such doctrine, and their defection left to Garrison only a fraction of the New England abolitionists. Clergymen of every creed publicly condemned "the sins of William Lloyd Garrison . . . his crusade against the churches—against the constitution and union of the United States—against civil government itself, with all its rights and powers"; and Garrison retorted with intolerant bitterness in the columns of the *Liberator*. The "blackhearted clergy," convinced that Garrison was a man "of whom honest men may well speak in terms of honest indignation," needed only leadership to crystallize its resentment into positive action against "Garrisonism" and all its works. That leadership was supplied by Lyman Beecher himself.

* * *

Congregational repudiation speeded the collapse of Garrison's support in New England. Reaction in Boston was so strong that not a church would open its doors to the next session of Garrison's society. Several abolitionist clergymen escaped the odium of Garrisonism by condemning Garrison and his heresies in a public statement, the Clerical Appeal. Claiming that their sentiments were shared by nine tenths of their fellow-workers in Massachusetts, they called upon abolitionists everywhere to repudiate Garrison and his *Liberator*. Raging with wounded vanity, Garrison demanded that the officers of the national society "punish this sedition and chastise" the authors of the document; but this they refused to do. Maddened by their "studied silence . . . respecting the Clerical Appeal," he wrote them again. "What is the meaning of it?" he asked. "I maintain, with all seriousness and earnestness, that you are both bound to meet these aspersions promptly, and in an official capacity; and should you refuse to do so, I for one shall feel that you will have greatly misapprehended your duty, and need to be admonished by abolitionists universally." He warned them that their silence, "if it be continued longer, will . . . call for a plain rebuke through the columns of the Liberator." Undisturbed by his threats of excommunication and abuse, however, the leaders refused to break their "studied silence"; though they did inform him by letter that in their opinion the charges in the Clerical Appeal were true.

But neither his proscription by the Congregational churches nor the alienation of his colleagues touched Garrison's conviction of his grandeur. He had no inkling that his conspicuousness in the movement was the work of those who called all abolitionists by his name in order to bring opprobrium upon the cause. The term "Garrisonism" was anything but an epithet of infamy to him; it was solid proof of leadership. Every such effort North and South to identify immediatism by his name only fed his self-esteem. Thus he viewed the Congregational resolutions as more than an assault upon his leadership. As the founder and embodiment of abolitionism, he considered his proscription by the clergy to be a proscription of the cause itself. "It is becoming more and more apparent," he wrote, that clergymen are "blind leaders of the blind, dumb dogs that cannot bark, spiritual popes—that they love the fleece better than the flock—that they are mighty hindrances to the cause of freedom." Abolitionism was not safe so long as clergymen were in control. *"The cause must be kept in the hands of laymen, or it will not be maintained."*

Garrison's terror of "the black-hearted clergy" was as much a delusion as was his certainty of his own primacy in the cause. From the beginning the movement had been inextricably bound up with the churches. The churches were its forums and the homes of its local organizations; from the churches it drew its justifying inspiration. It was an aspect of the churches, non-sectarian in organization but evangelical in character—a part of the benevolent empire. Everywhere in the organization clergymen were in control. Even in Garrison's own New England Anti-Slavery Society, clergymen composed nearly two thirds of the delegates in the typical session of 1835. In every aspect, the agitation was "a moral movement—a religious movement" drawing its life from the churches; and Garrison's "anticlerical" obsession made him an enemy of the antislavery impulse itself.

Amid the disintegrating elements of New England abolitionism, some still lingered in Garrison's train. His personal following was not inconsiderable. A few like Garrison had been dazzled by "the simplicity and beauty and consistency of the doctrine that all government, whether civil or ecclesiastical, conflicts with the government of Jehovah, and that by the Christian no other govt. can be acknowledged." Garrison did not originate his heresies. He merely caught up those "ultra views" of the 'thirties that rationalized his obsessions; and among abolitionists who were progressing toward the same opinions, his leadership was still unchanged.

Not all such followers were insignificant. There was Edmund Quincy, finished product of the Boston aristocracy, who left all to follow Garrison; and there was Wendell Phillips, "abolition's golden trumpet"; and there were others as able and devoted. But there were more who followed Garrison despite his heresies. They knew the man himself, the austerity of his life and his singleness of purpose. They knew that the harshness of his writings was derived from his righteous absolutes of faith, never from vindictiveness; and that his intolerance was for the principles that he hated, and not for the men who followed them. For all his "I-ness"—his obsessive self importance—Garrison was truly what his followers believed him to be, the embodiment of devotion to a cause.

Still to the public of the 'thirties, Garrison's harsh and intolerant style made up the man himself. If the hateful self-portrait which Garrison's own words depicted in the *Liberator* had been true, its effect could not have been more ruinous to the anti-slavery cause; for it was this picture that counted as Garrison with the public, and not Garrison himself. In the Eastern mind, he continued to be the incarnation of fanaticism, inimical to every institution of religion and the State.

The time had passed, however, when he could be "cashiered or voluntarily leave the ranks." The Garrison legend had been too long believed. To the thousands of distant abolitionists who knew nothing of his heresies, he was still "abolition personified and incarnate," and these would not sanction his repudiation. Though the Massachusetts society split apart and the movement in New England fell into hopeless disrepute, Garrison still remained a hero to his disciples and the legendary figure of abolitionism to the nation.

*   *   *

It was not Garrison's intention . . . that the American Anti-Slavery Society should dissolve. He regarded it as his own society, the child of his inspiration; and even its members, he reasoned, had no right to end its existence. He determined to save his society.

Garrison was perfectly aware that during the past year his support had largely evaporated. Indeed, except for the handful of "Garrison men" and certain of the former delegates to the Anti-Slavery Convention of American Women, he had no support worth mentioning anywhere in the organization. Among the delegates from the nation at the coming anniversary, he knew that he could expect nothing like a majority. He therefore decided to import a majority of his own! A steamboat was chartered and stationed at Lynn harbor, and citizens of Lynn were offered an outing to New York at nominal cost, on the understanding that they would cast their votes at Garrison's direction. "A large portion of the town of Lynn" responded, and were appointed "delegates." Similar methods were employed elsewhere, though the remainder of the "delegates" did not travel so picturesquely. More than five hundred of those who were enrolled in the anniversary of 1840 came from Massachusetts.

It was fortunate for Garrison that he had planned so well. Friends of the New York Committee had "drummed up recruits from all quarters," Garrison wrote his wife, "by the most dishonorable means." But their means fell short of the wholesale methods of the Bostonians. On a preliminary issue, the appointment of a woman to the business committee of the convention, women delegates and the town of Lynn joined hands. The New York Committee lost by a moderate majority (560 to 450), and rather than remain to be humiliated, they withdrew from the anniversary and the society. "It was our anti-slavery boat-load," Garrison boasted, "that saved our society from falling into the hands of the new organizers, or more correctly, disorganizers."

At last Garrison controlled "our society." Apparently he looked upon the anti-slavery boatload as an army of crusaders who had cleansed his own organization of rebels to his authority; and although their withdrawal left only Garrison's following as the convention, in his self-approving view this was as it should be. Nor was he disturbed when almost all of the state auxiliaries withdrew from the society. In his judgment, he was the society! But the departure of the auxiliaries left the American Anti-Slavery Society with little more than its name.

* * *

Once a year the Boston abolitionists invaded New York to hold the anniversary of the American Anti-Slavery Society. They printed no reports—there was nothing to report—and they discussed not at all the questions of budgets, pledges, and support which had concerned anniversaries in the past. Instead they elucidated points of doctrine and made speeches. Their doctrine now included no plan for emancipation. "To be without a plan," they said, "is the true genius and glory of the Anti-Slavery enterprise!" But their doctrine did include much that angered their contemporaries. They argued that the Constitution of the United States was "a covenant with death and an agreement with hell"; and the churches, they contended, were no better. On the other hand, their speeches, sometimes shocking and sometimes thrilling, but seldom dull, grew famous. Wendell Phillips spoke in polished periods amid hisses and applause, and Frederick Douglass uttered mighty words for freedom. The curious public thronged the anniversaries, and they were charged admission at the door. But only a handful of those who sat in the assemblies were members of the American Anti-Slavery Society; almost none were delegates. Indeed, there was no system of societies from which delegates could come. Behind this pretense of a national organization there was a total membership of only six hundred souls!

The anti-slavery impulse had departed, and hardly more than the name of the older movement still existed. But to Garrison the name and the impulse were still the same: he controlled the one and he was convinced that he embodied the other. At an anniversary meeting he proposed a resolution: "That indifference to this movement indicates a state of mind more culpable than was manifested by the Jewish nation in rejecting Jesus as the Messiah, eighteen hundred years ago"; and his loyal followers voted the resolution through.

Since the schism in the Massachusetts Society, these followers of Garrison had come to constitute a fraternity—almost a secret society —based upon the knowledge, mutually shared, that Garrison was not the egregious fanatic of his public reputation, but a single-minded hero—"the only man who *would do to tie to*," as Thomas Wentworth Higginson said. Their faithfulness was astonishing but not incredible. Garrison's conviction of his own significance gave to those who shared it that unclouded sense of right which has been one of the chief consolations of religion through the ages. To others, his integrity and consistency were enough to hold their loyalty. But all told, they were few. So far as their influence goes in history, their primary function was to sustain the legend that Garrison and the abolition cause were one. The popular tradition that Garrison had first inspired the anti-slavery impulse, they kept alive by constant iteration; and though they were now even further than before from the actual center of the movement, they still maintained that Garrison was its chief. Thus they claimed for him the glory of each victory that others won in the anti-slavery struggle; and hostile publicists, ready to damn the anti-slavery cause with every odious epithet, gladly ratified their claim. In time, sheer repetition made their legend of Garrison's leadership a part of our tradition.

Not all of those who ratified the legend were hostile to the cause. Notables of New England, knowing Garrison as a voice at their literary afternoons in Boston rather than as the evil genius of the anti-slavery movement, found in his lofty qualities of consistency and devotion a character not incongruous with the legend. Moreover, even the greatest of them knew little enough of the Methodists and Baptists who formed the bulk of New England abolition, and they knew even less of the tens of thousands of abolitionists who made up the movement in the nation. Thus, with no basis for a sounder judgment, they accepted Garrison at his own valuation, and embalmed the legend of his leadership in the New England literary tradition.

The Boston abolitionists made the Garrison legend history; but this was their only great achievement. As advocates for a reputation, Garrison's followers were unique; but as factors in the anti-slavery impulse —at least throughout the decade of the 'forties—they and their leader were even less than negligible; they were "dead weights to the abolition cause."

24

Russel B. Nye (1955)[1]

*A re-evaluation of Garrison began in the 1950's,
when historians like Ralph Korngold and Russel Nye laid the
basis for a more favorable image. No doubt this was due in part
to the crisis on Civil Rights and to changing attitudes toward
the Negro and his place in American society. Garrison suddenly
seemed to have something to offer. What is presented here to
illustrate the shift in attitude is the major portion of Nye's epi-
logue to his short biography* William Lloyd Garrison and the
Humanitarian Reformers. *This is a well-balanced and vivid
assessment of Garrison's thought and behavior. Nye, it will be
noted, describes Garrison much more sympathetically than does
Barnes, but he accepts Barnes's view of Garrison's marginality
in the organized antislavery movement. He goes on to contend,
however, that Garrison's "symbolic" quality for both the South
and the North makes him a key to the Civil War crisis.*

Garrison's mind worked on two levels, the moral and the practical. On the one, his approach to issues was determined by principle;
on the other, by tactics and strategy. The level of his argument fluctu-
ated, as it did during the Civil War when he scourged Lincoln on
principles, yet pleaded the value of expediency. Fundamentally, his
approach to things was simple and consistent. He judged everything
by two standards of moral right—natural law as expressed in the
Declaration of Independence, and Christian ethic as expressed in the
Bible. To him these were essentially one, emanating from the same
divine source. Any idea or institution which violated either, in part
or whole, therefore was wrong. The final judgment rested with individual conscience, the roots of which lay in God. A world of conscience so rooted was Garrison's "kingdom to be established on earth,"

[1] From Russel B. Nye, *William Lloyd Garrison and the Humanitarian Reformers*
(Boston, 1955), pp. 198–206. Copyright © 1955 by Russel B. Nye. Reprinted by
permission of Little, Brown and Company.

in which the individual's own soul became the arbiter of action and the judge of institutions—a kingdom in which men voluntarily ceased to sin, established justice, and worshiped God in a "magistracy of holiness and love."

The central fact of Garrison's life was his religious faith. The Bible was the only book he ever really read, and his abolitionism itself sprang directly from his belief that slavery violated God's law. "It was not on account of your complexion or race, as a people, that I espoused your cause," he told a Negro meeting in Charleston in 1865, "but because you were the children of a common Father, created in the same divine image, having the same inalienable rights. . . ." Despite the charge of "infidelity" that followed him wherever he went, he was a rigidly religious man. The bland neutrality of nineteenth-century Unitarianism was not for him. The finespun speculations of New England transcendentalism lay beyond his capacity; even Lyman Beecher's brand of modified Calvinism was too soft. Instead he returned to an earlier, rigorous faith, straight from his Bible. In 1842, stung to exasperation by accusations of "infidelity," he published his creed in the *Liberator:*

> I believe that, in Jesus Christ, the believer is dead unto sin, and alive with God—that whosoever is born of God overcometh the world —that Christ is the end of the law for righteousness, to everyone who believeth. . . . I believe that priestcraft, and sectarianism, and slavery, and war, and everything that defileth or maketh a lie, are of the devil, and destined to an eternal overthrow.

The language was the language of the Old Testament, the spirit that of third-century Christianity. He had the zeal and fanaticism of a Biblical prophet, combined with apostolic dedication. His religion, he said, was "that of the Jewish religionists of eighteen centuries ago," and his God a Hebraic God who spoke directly to his conscience. Him and only Him would Garrison obey and call Master.

From this Godbased individualism flowed Garrison's revolt against manmade authority—abolition, disunion, pacifism, perfectionism, women's rights, and "infidelity." "Individual, personal effort"—he wrote—

> is the true foundation of all real prosperity in the social state, and all excellence of character. No form of Society can be devised which will

release the individual from personal responsibility. . . . It would be the greatest curse that could be inflicted upon him.

Garrison thus did not belong in an age of conciliation and compromise, nor was he fitted for what his era called "the principle of association." He liked, he said, "causes which, being righteous, are unpopular, and struggling, in God's name, against wind and tide." With God and conscience on his side, turmoil was his natural element. "Hisses," he once said, "are music to my ears." Organizations strait-jacketed him; he accepted them only as utensils for his own use. Temperamentally he was a no-government man and his aversion to cooperation was as ingrained as Thoreau's.

Garrison was a true revolutionary individualist who accepted nothing beyond himself, no tradition or institution whose existence violated his own inner, higher law. There was something of the eighteenth-century rebel in him, and more of the seventeenth-century Puritan's self-righteous independence. Emerson, too, preached the sufficiency of self and the integrity of self-reliance as God-reliance, but Garrison's deity was no transcendental Oversoul. His was a stern, inflexible God of wrath and justice, his individualism a flinty, arrogant self-faith. Emerson's individualism was ascetic and intellectual; Garrison's was visceral, emotional. He could never have taken to the woods as Thoreau did. He was a social being, tied to humanity and incapable of acting without it. As Emerson shrewdly remarked, Garrison "would find nothing to do in a lonely world, or a world with half-a-dozen inhabitants."

Acting from his own driving religious faith and within the terms of his society, Garrison had every reason to be what he was—the Reformer Incarnate. He conceived himself to be the tool of God, his followers "soldiers of God" with "loins girt about with truth" and "feet shod with the preparation of the Gospel of peace." His aim was nothing less than "the emancipation of our whole race from the dominion of man, from the thraldom of self, from the government of brute force, from the bondage of sin." This was the New Jerusalem, the kingdom of God awaited by the Hebrew prophets. The complete freedom of man was to him the whole purpose of life, and he lived with singleminded devotion to it.

Those who accused Garrison of deserting the main battle of abolition for minor skirmishes failed to recognize that to Garrison no reform, however close to the lunatic fringe, was unrelated to the larger purpose. He was always, as he said late in life, interested in nothing less than "the redemption of the human race." If the human race needed redemption from slavery on the one hand and cigar-smoking on the other, there was no reason to neglect one crusade for another if both could proceed at once. Bronson Alcott, of all Garrison's contemporaries, understood the grand sweep of his design and saw what the others missed. He was, Alcott wrote in his journal, wholly "intent on the melioration of human woes and the eradication of human evils." Nothing else could satisfy him. Garrison was no intellectual, but a man of action. He never liked to speculate, and he had no reverence for reflection. Emerson once said that Garrison "neighed like a horse" when they discussed ideas. Unlike Emerson, Garrison never tried to search hard for truth, because he had it.

The moral self-righteousness that lay beneath Garrison's crusade for the kingdom of God on earth was difficult to accept. There was no vacillation in him, no gray in his thinking, only right and wrong, deep black and pure white. There could be no compromise with sin and only Garrison could define sin. To disagree with him was to disagree with Right personified. In the last analysis his final court of appeal was conscience, not mind. Moral judgment was his first and last line of defense, and for this reason it was almost impossible to persuade him he was wrong. Founded on God and conscience, his stand was impregnable.

This absolute self-confidence was one reason his band followed him with worship this side of idolatry. Garrison had no hesitations, no questionings, no doubts, and inspired the same self-assurance in others. His sincerity and courage attracted men so widely different as the gentle May, the urbane Phillips, the wildly unstable Foster, and the unpredictable Wright. Some of his twists and turns made his most ardent supporters swallow hard, but Garrison to the end of his life believed himself perfectly consistent and unassailably right. His enemies always respected his obstinate sincerity. They sometimes thought he was wrong, or arrogant, or unreasonable—but never insincere. He was capable of absolute identification with a principle. If he believed in an idea he would die for it, though it be ill-advised, wrong, or downright foolish. This monolithic self-confidence drew men to him.

Garrison's faith in himself made him unconsciously dictatorial. He genuinely considered himself a modest man, refusing personal praise and credit. Yet he constantly sought it with a real inward hunger.

His personality felt a deep need for recognition. He never aspired to political office, though certainly after 1861 he could have had it. He paid little attention to money, security, or possessions. He simply neglected to write his memoirs when he could have made thousands, and the financial status of the *Liberator* was always more important to him than his own. But he was sure from the first that he was a man for the ages, and he felt compelled to keep reminding himself and others of the fact. His remarks in the *Liberator,* less than a year after its inception, were not those of a humble, self-effacing young man: "The present generation cannot appreciate the purity of my motives or the value of my exertions. I look to posterity for a good reputation. The unborn offspring of those who are now living will reverse the condemnatory decision of my contemporaries." Again, a few months later, he turned to a companion on leaving a meeting to remark, "You may someday write my biography."

Garrison was not averse to comparing himself to the Apostles, though he obviously possessed little of their patience and forbearance. He rarely forgot or forgave those who differed with him, and occasionally he took more credit where less was due without the slightest embarrassment. He had not, as Alcott put it trenchantly, "won those self-victories which lead to the superior powers of those who have won themselves." Significantly, Garrison had only a limited circle of close friends—"God's choreboy" Samuel May, Johnson, Quincy, and, closest of all, George Thompson, a man much like himself. Garrison lived in terms of his future epitaph, and carried his own Westminster Abbey about with him.

William Lloyd Garrison's place in history was hotly debated in his own time. His admirers made him a greater man than he was, and his opponents gave him less praise than he deserved. According to Wendell Phillips, Garrison "began, inspired, and largely controlled" the entire abolition movement from beginning to end. Another idolator called him "lawgiver at Washington, inspirer of Presidential policy, and framer of the greatest war of modern times." But William Birney regarded Garrisonism as "the most utter abortion known in the history of this country," and Henry Ward Beecher characterized him as "no more than a blister" on the antislavery movement. Neither the Tappans, nor Birney, nor Lundy, nor Weld, nor any of the pioneer abolitionists beyond New England thought of Garrison as more than an intractable, disturbing though sincere and devoted co-worker whose misguided zeal sometimes brought more harm than good to the cause.

The Garrison legend was partly the result of reams of uncritical praise poured out by Garrisonians—May, Johnson, Phillips, and others—in contrast to the comparative silence of those who opposed him. More than a little of Garrison's own conviction of immortality rubbed off on his followers. "Garrison has an army of men to write him up," said E. L. Pierce in 1892, "and his writers are unscrupulous." Those who admired Garrison gloried in praising him; those who opposed him charitably kept quiet.

It is only fair to grant Garrison pre-eminence in the first decade of abolition agitation. He personified its aggressive phase, publicized it for better or worse, and drove its issues deep into the national conscience. But he did not begin abolitionism, nor did he organize it. Weld and the Westerners, and the Tappans and the New Yorkers, deserve a large share of the credit; had Garrison never existed things might have been much the same. The movement, set in motion by others, was carried to its conclusion by methods he could not accept and ideas he could not understand. Abolition passed through him, not from him.

Yet Garrison was a person of real historical importance, for he was a symbol to his generation of the moral and ideological conflict that took its final shape in the Civil War. To the South, he represented all that was baleful and dangerous. Whatever his insistence on pacific intentions, he stirred up violent resentments and his appeals reached the passions rather than the consciences of slaveholders. His principle of "moral agitation" against slavery created only agitation. The proslavery forces, already consolidating, could concentrate all their fear and anger on him. If the approaching conflict was irrepressible, Garrison was at least a factor in convincing the South that it was so. By proslavery logic, Garrison led to John Brown; Brown led to Lincoln; Garrison, Brown, and Lincoln together led to an intolerable conclusion. It was easier for the South to argue from personalities rather than from principles, and Garrison was a personality no Southerner could overlook. By very little effort of his own he became a bogeyman to the South and a personification to it of things to come.

To the North, Garrison was a goad, a prick to the conscience, a symbol of the moral problem of slavery that remained unsolved despite compromises, conciliations, and tacit agreements to disregard it. Slavery, no matter how it was explained or rationalized, *did* exist; the fact of its existence *was* an anomaly in a nation dedicated to life, liberty, and the individual's right to pursue happiness. Garrison, more than any other one person, shattered the "conspiracy of silence." One might decry his invective, censure his methods, or deny his appeal to disorder; one could never shut out his clamor. To disagree with Garrison men had to face up to the problem, rethink their beliefs, examine their own consciences. When men did this, slavery was doomed. Garrison contributed relatively little to the philosophy of abolitionism. He had only a single thought—that "slavery was a crime, a damning crime"—but he made other men think, though he sometimes muddled their thinking. Economic and political events that Garrison neither knew nor cared about made slavery a national issue and precipitated the war. But it had its moral causes too, which Garrison's career aptly symbolized to the victorious North.

25
John L. Thomas (1963)[1]

The closest approach to a definitive biography of Garrison is John L. Thomas's The Liberator, published in 1963. Thomas's view is a complex one and suggests the difficulties involved in a modern rehabilitation of Garrison. Thomas is in sympathy with the antislavery cause but cannot ignore what he describes as the "authoritarian" side of Garrison's personality. He feels obliged to judge Garrison rather severely for the tactical decisions that resulted from his doctrinaire "perfectionist" philosophy of reform. If Thomas is critical of Garrison, he is nevertheless free of the belittling tendency to dismiss Garrison as unimportant or to ascribe his thinking to individual peculiarities. He makes a strong case against the Barnes thesis that the Western antislavery movement developed independently of Garrison's influence and example by showing that Theodore Weld was converted to abolition in 1832 by men who had themselves been won to the cause by Garrison's Thoughts on African Colonization. Thomas has also provided a perceptive discussion of the growth of Garrison's perfectionist approach to politics that gives more emphasis to a cultural situation conducive to such thinking than to any peculiar traits Garrison might have had. The selection that follows is the book's summary and conclusion.

When Garrison died in 1879, Reconstruction had already ended with Northern assent to the subordination of the Southern Negro. Slavery was dead, but racial inequality and the belief in the inferiority of the black man lived on. The Civil War had proved a limited victory that preserved the Union but intensified race conflict, freed the slaves but returned them to the management of their former masters. Beset by the new doubts of a Darwinian age, the postwar generation began to reassess the idea of human perfectibility and the

[1] From John L. Thomas, *The Liberator: William Lloyd Garrison* (Boston, 1963), pp. 452–59. Copyright © 1963 by John L. Thomas. Reprinted by permission of Little, Brown and Company.

message of liberation it had taught. Gradually the simple, buoyant faith in the perfectibility of man was giving way to a more sophisticated theory of evolution. Yet is was this belief in natural moral goodness—perfectionism—which had formed the credo of ante-bellum America, provided the driving force of the anti-slavery movement, and sustained the pitch of Garrison's reform. It had also caused a war.

All Americans before the Civil War shared in the perfectionist dream in some way, for perfectionism promised the country a perpetually renewable innocence and vigor. Perfectionism meant freedom —freedom from sin and guilt, freedom from the past and the burdens of history, freedom from institutions and power. What had Europe with its decadence and corruption to teach a young America? Left alone to flourish, the New World would produce a new race of men strong in their natural goodness and their commitment to total freedom. Perfectionism verified the American belief in the second chance.

The signs of this perfectionist faith were everywhere in ante-bellum America: in the physical fact of the frontier; in the Jacksonian bias against institutions and corporate power; in the pervasive sense of the civilizing mission of Americans; in the concept of nature as a regenerative experience; in the legends and folklore of the people. There were two principal sources of American perfectionism: the Enlightenment tradition of the American Revolution and the pietism of evangelical religion, the first a secular belief in progress transplanted from Europe, the second a millennial expectation at the heart of American revivalism. Combined, these two powerful ideals of infinite progress and the equality of souls made an explosive compound of moral idealism. It was this idealism which the abolitionists discovered they shared with the people and which gave their argument its peculiarly effective appeal.

The anti-slavery movement itself sprang from a religious impulse and advanced with the Second Great Awakening; that is, it originated in a religious revival and remained primarily a religious crusade. Since it was chiefly Christian in its emphasis, it was subject to the two great polar forces in Christian thought—the pull of pietism and the stress of social ethics. Pietism emphasizes the devotional ideal of religion, the desire for salvation and the achievement of holiness. Christian ethics, on the contrary, postulates a community and the good life to be lived within it. Pietism tends to be sectarian, mystical, perfectionist. It concentrates on the regenerative relation between God and the individual, on the inner experience of divine power. Thus it tends to be anti-institutional and ascetic. By stressing the role of the individual conscience and making obedience to it the highest form of duty, it gives the true believer a new freedom from the rules and regulations of the world; but in stressing the idea of purity it is apt to be rigoristic and exclusive. The idea of a social ethic is in many ways its exact opposite—adaptable, humanistic, inclusive, an ideal of Christian life that takes account of organization and power.

Both of these forces were at work within the anti-slavery movement from the beginning. The abolitionists knew very little about the institution of slavery. They approached the problem from the direction of regenerative experience through the avenue of conversion. Their strong Protestant individualism led them to treat slavery not simply as an inefficient labor system but as a betrayal of Christian values. They believed that slavery was inhuman because it denied God to the black man. They viewed slavery as a moral problem. It was not long, however, before some of them discovered the institutional complexities of the slavery problem. There were those like Garrison and his followers who persistently ignored these questions, but there were also those abolitionists like Birney, Stanton, and Leavitt who recognized the need for organization and policy. As the anti-slavery enterprise grew it was exposed to the same tension between piety and ethics as its parent Christianity.

The original American Anti-Slavery Society was both a sect and a church, a closed society of faithful saints and a wider community embracing all the people. Garrison's Declaration of Sentiments exemplified the underlying ambiguity of the anti-slavery program: it promised political action but enjoined moral reform; it demanded immediate emancipation but failed to define it; it preached pacifism but appealed to passion. Within a decade these twin forces had produced divergent strains of anti-slavery, one based on political action, the other on moral preaching. Both groups of abolitionists claimed that their program was the only true one, and each accused the other of abandoning the slave. Both were wrong. In reality, each group embodied an aspect of the abolitionist temperament and the religious mind, and each in its own way illustrated the problems of religious idealism and defined the limits of Christian reform.

Both of these Christian strains found expression in William Lloyd Garrison. He wanted to abolish slavery and make a better world, but even more he wanted to avoid contamination by keeping his own hands clean. In the face of mounting evidence to the contrary he clung to the illusion that antislavery and pacifism were not merely compatible but complementary. Most of the abolitionists had indulged in this hope in the beginning, but it did not take long to undeceive them. Garrison, however, refused to give up the fiction of peaceful revolution. Until the actual outbreak of war he declined to admit that a situation might arise which would require him to choose between peace and freedom for the slave. The Civil War may not have been inevitable, but after the Compromise of 1850 a peaceful solution to slavery grew less likely each day. It was just this fact that his critics tried to tell him—that the pressure of events operating independently of the will of the majority of Americans was dividing the country and making his prophecy of disunion come true. Garrison failed to understand the very forces he had let loose. For thirty years he cried havoc, and when it came, he refused to credit it and contented himself with his prophet's role, rousing the emotion of Northerners and Southerners yet disavowing their actions, creating an atmosphere of unreason and ignoring the consequences. In his uncompromising stand against both slavery and politics he personifies the great strength and the equally great weakness of radical reform.

The radical reformer in American politics has been something of a split personality, a nonconformist with authoritarian leanings who presents the community with a dilemma by recalling it to its ideals and rejecting its arguments for order and stability. In the strength of his nonconformity Garrison contributed significantly to an American tradition concerned with the integrity of minorities and the protection of civil liberties. His anti-slavery career illustrates the importance of minorities in a free society, the need to withstand the pressure for conformity exerted by society and the willingness to be beaten rather than give hostages to majority opinion. Garrison believed that in the long run respect for law mattered less than concern for right. He considered politics dirty business and looked on the man of average goodness as an enemy in disguise. With his convictions of racial equality, his iron determination in the face of overwhelming opposition, and his insistence on the right to hold and preach unpopular opinions he has a strong claim on the American liberal tradition.

Nonconformity, however, is only one aspect of the radical temperament, and it was only a part of Garrison's mind. The other was distinctly authoritarian. Impulsive yet distrustful, seeking support but rejecting it when given, aggressive and undisciplined, demanding obedience but unable to accept it, he lacked the knowledge of men and the world that makes for leadership. His organization suffered grievously from his failings. When he did not try to do everything himself, he grudgingly delegated a task to a follower and then treated him as a threat to his ascendancy. His societies remained small because he refused to share power and tolerate possible rivals. Because he also lacked any administrative sense he convinced himself that it was unnecessary. His meetings and conventions were like religious revivals, spontaneous and disorganized, and the *Liberator* especially suffered from his lack of method. The man who demanded order and authority in the new world he was making could not find it in his own life. His view of the world as a vast arena for the struggle between God and the devil, his tenacious anti-intellectualism, and above all, his vision of a perfect and self-regulating society of saints disclosed the longings of an authoritarian mind concerned with getting and using power over others.

Inevitably the contradiction in Garrison's personality colored the cause to which he gave himself. Orestes Brownson, a tireless joiner of causes in his own right but also a shrewd observer, identified this contradiction when he noted that Garrison and the anti-slavery men had no just claim to the American civil rights tradition. "Moreover," he added, "the abolitionists do not, properly speaking, discuss the subject of slavery. Nay, it is not their object to discuss it. Their object is not to enlighten the community on the subject, but to agitate it. . . . *When men have made up their minds,* when the epoch for deliberation has gone by, and that for action has come, when their object is less to convince than it is to rouse, to quicken, to inflame; then proceedings like those of the abolitionists are very appropriate."

The abolitionists *had* made up their minds; they never doubted for a moment that slavery was wrong. Despite the complaints of Brownson and other critics, they succeeded in identifying their cause with the life of free society. They were the carriers, however unworthy at times, of perfectionism and the ideals of democracy. They invoked the freedoms guaranteed by the Constitution and demanded that the people honor them and listen to their arguments. Yet their arguments, as Brownson quite rightly pointed out, were not the kind that could be discussed dispassionately. Their ideas were packed with high explosive and eventually destroyed a community based on slavery. The abolitionists found the majority wrong and demanded the liberty to say so. The liberty that Garrison and his followers dreamed of, however, was an absolute liberty, a freedom that was neither brotherly nor Christian. It was this subversive ideal of liberty which, despite their professions of peace and Christian love, led logically to war and the overthrow of slavery.

This contradiction in the anti-slavery attitude was expressed on a higher level in the changes Garrison and the abolitionists made in the doctrine of natural law. As they received it from the Declaration of Independence and first invoked it in self-defense, natural law meant a body of rights pragmatically determined and consonant with what was believed to be the nature of man. In the course of their fight against slavery the abolitionists changed the content while keeping the concept. Natural law, as Garrison came to use it, meant metaphysical truth, a divine spirit hovering over humanity. For the pragmatic Aristotelian they substituted a Christian faith in a universally valid spiritual criterion. Drained of its pragmatic content, natural law came to mean, as Justice Holmes once observed, anything that people are willing to fight for. The Civil War proved that the American people were willing to fight over slavery.

The anti-slavery persuasion was marked by a final contradiction which was the source of the abolitionists' great strength and tragic weakness. Their courage and their fierce sense of freedom blinded them to the realities of the power struggle and the consequences of freeing the slave. The very intensity of their belief prevented them from understanding fully what it lay in their power to do for the Negro. They welcomed emancipation, but they were not ready for it and did not know how to use it. With the actual freeing of the slave their lack of understanding became increasingly apparent until finally anti-slavery radicalism broke down.

If Garrison personifies the contradictions of American radical reform, his anti-slavery career illustrates the continuing problem of moral absolutes in a democracy. A free society needs radicals with their moral absolutes just as ante-bellum Americans needed the abolitionists to tell them that slavery was wrong. But perfectionism—the dream of a perfect society of regenerate men—which sustained Garrison and his followers, rejected democratic politics and the idea of compromise, ignored programs and plans. By concentrating almost exclusively on the moral issue, appealing directly to individuals, and demanding immediate and wholesale change, it eliminated the very possibility of controlled change. Without radicals to criticize it a democracy is not really free; with them it maintains a precarious existence. If it cannot afford to silence its critics, neither can American democracy ignore the dangers to its stability inherent in their insistent demand for a better world.

"In every great fluctuation that takes place in human society," John Jay Chapman wrote of Garrison and the Civil War, "—whether it be a moral, a political, or even an industrial phenomenon,—force converges upon some one man, and makes him the metaphysical center and thought-focus of the movement." Chapman was not equipped to probe the collective mind of ante-bellum America: the grandson of an abolitionist, he was too close temporally and temperamentally to the Emersonian Representative Man to see Garrison as he was. Garrison was not a heroic figure but, rather, Emerson's sufficient man, "an officer equal to his task." He knew the contradictions of his age experientially, which is to say that his weakness was in a sense an American weakness. He lacked the power of a leader and the sureness to shape his feelings and give direction to his beliefs. Not a Representative Man, he was yet a representative figure of American society before the Civil War whose single great achievement and equally great failure testify to the tragic meaning of history.

26
Howard Zinn (1965)[1]

Thomas's book, although widely praised, was not received with universal favor. Some historians of the neo-abolitionist persuasion felt that he was too hard on Garrison and that a much more complimentary portrait could be drawn. As yet, no historian has provided an authoritative, across-the-board defense of Garrison as the great American radical. The outlines of such an interpretation are apparent, however, in the following excerpts from an essay by Howard Zinn, a political scientist with a vital interest in contemporary Civil Rights activity.

"Extremist" carries a psychological burden when attached to political movements, which it does not bear in other situations. A woman who is extremely beautiful, a man who is extremely kind, a mechanic who is extremely skillful, a child who is extremely healthy—these represent laudable ideals. In politics, however, the label "extremist" carries unfavorable implications. It may mean that the person desires a change in the status quo which is more sweeping than that requested by most people. For instance, in a period when most people are willing to free the slaves, but not to enfranchise them, one wanting to give them equal rights would be considered an extremist. Or it may mean someone who urges a more drastic action to attain a goal shared by most people; that is, someone who advocates slave revolts (like John Brown) rather than compensated emancipation followed by colonization abroad (like Lincoln).

Yet, in any given political situation, there is a very large number of possible alternatives, both in desired goals and in the means of achieving them. The actual alternatives put forward in any one situation are usually much fewer than the total range of possibilities.

[1] From Howard Zinn, "Abolitionists, Freedom-Riders, and the Tactics of Agitation," in *The Antislavery Vanguard: New Essays on the Abolitionists,* ed. Martin Duberman (Princeton, 1965), pp. 421–26, *passim,* pp. 432–37. Reprinted by permission of Princeton University Press.

And the most extreme suggestion put forward at the time will be labeled "extremist" even though it may be far less sweeping than other possible courses of action.

For instance, William Lloyd Garrison, looked upon both by his antagonists and by modern historians as an "extremist," did not seek goals as far-reaching as he might have. He explained, around 1830, his stand for "immediate abolition" as follows: "Immediate abolition does not mean that the slaves shall immediately exercise the right of suffrage, or be eligible to any office, or be emancipated from law, or be free from the benevolent restraints of guardianship." Yet the ideas of suffrage and office-holding were not too much for Thaddeus Stevens and Charles Sumner—nor for Garrison—in 1865, when actual freedom had come for the slaves. . . .

The point is, that we are not precise in our standards for measuring "extremism." We do not take into account all possible alternatives, in either goal or method, which may be more extreme than the one we are so labeling. This leads writers to call "extreme" any proposal more drastic than that favored by the majority of articulate people at the time (or by the writer). In a society where the word "extreme" has a bad connotation, in a literate community enamored by the Aristotelian golden mean, we often hurl that word unjustifiably at some proposal which is extreme only in a context of limited alternatives. . . .

If the notion of "extremism" is too nebulous to sustain a firm judgment on a goal or a tactic, how do we judge? One point of reference might be the nature and severity of the problem. Even that moderate, Lao Tzu, said you use a boat for a stream and a litter for a mountain path; you adapt your means to your problem. While more modest evils might be dislodged by a few sharp words, the elimination of slavery clearly required more drastic action. The abolitionists did not deceive themselves that they were gentle and temperate; they quite consciously measured their words to the enormity of the evil.

Garrison said in 1833: "How, then, ought I to feel and speak and write, in view of a system which is red with innocent blood drawn from the bodies of millions of my countrymen by the scourge of brutal drivers. . . . My soul should be, as it is, on fire. I should thunder, I should lighten, I should blow the trumpet of alarm long and loud.

I should use just such language as is most descriptive of the crime."

How evil was slavery? It was a complex phenomenon, different in every individual instance, with the treatment of slaves varying widely. But the whole range of variation was in a general framework of unspeakable inhumanity. Even at its "best," slavery was a ferocious attack on man's dignity. It was described matter-of-factly by a supporter of the system, Judge Edmund Ruffin of North Carolina: "Such services can only be expected from one who has no will of his own; who surrenders his will in implicit obedience to another. Such obedience is the consequence only of uncontrolled authority over the body. There is no remedy. This discipline belongs to the state of slavery. . . . It constitutes the curse of slavery to both the bond and the free portion of our population. But it is inherent in the relation of master and slave."

And at its worst, slavery was, as Allan Nevins has said: ". . . the greatest misery, the greatest wrong, the greatest curse to white and black alike that America has ever known." Ads for fugitive slaves in the Southern press (5,400 advertisements a year) contained descriptions like the following to aid apprehension:

> . . . Stamped N.E. on the breast and having both small toes cut off. . . . Has some scars on his back that show above the skin, caused by the whip. . . . Has an iron band around his neck. . . . Has a ring of iron on his left foot. . . . Has on a large neck iron, with a huge pair of horns and a large bar or band of iron on his left leg. . . . Branded on the left cheek, thus "R", and a piece is taken off her left ear on the same side; the same letter is branded on the inside of both legs.

One plantation diary read: ". . . whipped every field hand this evening." A Natchez slave who attacked a white man was chained to a tree and burned alive.

Against this, how mild Garrison's words seem.

*　　*　　*

The argument over the wisdom of radical agitation in the tactics of social reform was aptly expressed in Boston in pre-Civil War years by two leading figures. Samuel May, speaking of Garrison, said: ". . . he will shake our nation to its center, but he will shake slavery out of it." Reverend Lyman Beecher said: "True wisdom consists in advocating a cause only so far as the community will sustain the reformer." The agitator, declare the moderate reformers, shakes so hard that he makes compromise impossible, alienates friends, and delays rather than speeds the coming of reform.

Compromise was not disdained by the abolitionists; they were fully conscious of the fact that the outcome of any social struggle is almost always some form of compromise. But they were also aware of that which every intelligent radical knows: that to compromise in advance is to vitiate at the outset that power for progress which only the radical propels into the debate. Lowell put this most vividly, declaring that the abolitionists "are looked upon as peculiarly ungrateful and impracticable if they do not devote their entire energies to soliciting nothing, and express a thankfulness amounting almost to rapture when they get it."

The abolitionist took an advanced position so that even if pushed back by compromise, substantial progress would result. Garrison wrote: "Urge immediate abolition as earnestly as we may, it will be gradual abolition in the end." And Phillips said: "If we would get half a loaf, we must demand the whole of it." The Emancipation Proclamation itself was a compromise, the tortured product of a long battle between radicals and moderates in and out of the Lincoln administration, and only the compelling force of the abolitionist intransigeants made it come as soon as it did.

Two factors demand recognition by moderates who disdain "extreme" positions on the ground that compromise is necessary. One is the above-mentioned point that the early projection of an advanced position ensures a compromise on more favorable terms than would be the case where the timorous reformer compromises at the start (in which case the result is a compromise upon a compromise, since he will be forced to retreat even from his retreat after all the forces are calculated at the social weighing-in). The other is that there is a huge difference between the passive wisher-for-change who quietly adds up the vectors and makes a decision as to which is the composite of all existing forces, and the active reformer who pushes so hard *in the course of adding-up* that the composite itself is changed. The latter—the radical—is viewing compromise as a dynamic process, in which his own actions are part of the total force being calculated. He bases his estimate of what is possible on a graph in which his own action and its consequences are calculated from the first.

MODERATION AS A TACTIC

Does the agitator alienate potential allies by the extremism of his demands, or the harshness of his language? Lewis Tappan, the wealthy New Yorker who financed many abolitionist activities, wrote anxiously to George Thompson, the British abolitionist: "The fact need not be concealed from you that several emancipationists so disapprove of the harsh, and, as they think, the unchristian language of *The Liberator*, that they do not feel justified in upholding it." This, in general, was the feeling of the Executive Committee of the American Anti-Slavery Society in the early years of the movement. Undoubtedly, the Society itself was not diverted from its aim of abolishing slavery because of Garrison's immoderation; they were concerned lest others be alienated.

But who? The slaveholder? The slave? The moderate reformer? The open-minded conservative? It needs to be acknowledged that different sections of the population will respond differently to the same appeal, and in judging the effect of bold words upon the population, this population must be broken up into parts, based on the varying degrees of receptivity to the ideas of the reformer. Why should the radical soften his language or his program to please that element of the population which cannot possibly be pleased by anything short of total surrender of principle, whose self-interest in fact dictates rejection of any reform? Lowell wrote: "The slaveholder, when Mr. Greeley would politely request him to state what method would be most consonant to his feelings, would answer, as did the . . . boy whose mother asked him what he would like for breakfast, 'Just what you ain't gut!' "

Only the hypothesis of common interest for the entire population can justify an appeal to the opponent on the basis of reason, asking him to perceive his interest more accurately. But if in fact there is a diversity of interest, then the lighting up of the truth can only bring out more sharply that conflict which stands in the way of agreement. The slaveholders themselves pointed to the impossibility of their being won over by moderate overtures. In 1854, the editor of the Richmond *Enquirer*, wrote: "That man must be a veritable verdigreen who dreams of pleasing slaveholders, either in church or state, by any method but that of letting slavery alone." William Ellery Channing tried such appeal and failed. One of his brochures against slavery was so mild that some described it as putting people to sleep, but he was abused so harshly it might as well have been one of Garrison's flame-breathing *Liberator* editorials.

With a population of diversified interests, tactics must be adapted and focused specially for each group, and for the group most inimical to reform, it is doubtful that moderation is effective. With the in-transigeants, it may be only the most powerful action that impels change. It was Nat Turner's violent slave revolt in Virginia in 1831 that led the Virginia legislature into its famous series of discussions about the abolition of slavery. "For a while indeed," Ralph Korngold writes, "it seemed that what years of propaganda by the Quakers had failed to accomplish would come as a result of Turner's bloodletting."

When friends of the reformers rail against harsh words or strong action (as the American Anti-Slavery Society did against Garrison) it is clear that they themselves will not be put off from reform because of it, but fear the effects on others. And if neither extreme opposition nor hard-and-fast friends can be moved by tactics of moderation, this leaves, as a decisive group, that large part of the population which is at neither end of the ideological spectrum, which moves back and forth across the center line, depending on circumstances.

Garrison was quite aware that most of the American population to which he was appealing was not sympathetic with his views, and he was completely conscious of how distant were his own fiery convictions from those of the average American. But he was persuaded, as were Phillips and other leading abolitionists (John Brown felt it, and acted it, if he did not express it intellectually) that only powerful surges of words and feelings could move white people from their complacency about the slave question. He said once in Philadelphia: "Sir, slavery will not be overthrown without excitement, a most tremendous excitement." He must lash with words, he felt, those Americans who had never felt the whip of a slaveowner. To his friend Samuel May, who urged him to keep more cool, saying: "Why, you are all on fire," Garrison replied: "Brother May, I have need to be all on fire, for I have mountains of ice about me to melt."

We have the historical record as a check on whether the vituperative language of Garrison, the intemperate appeals of Wendell Phillips, hurt or advanced the popular sentiment against slavery. In the 1830's a handful of men cried out against slavery and were beaten, stoned, and shot to death by their Northern compatriots. By 1849, antislavery sentiment was clearly increasing, and some of the greatest minds and voices in America were speaking out for abolition. Lowell asked curtly of those who charged the abolitionists with retarding the movement: ". . . has there really been a change of public opinion for the worse, either at the North or the South, since the *Liberator* came into existence eighteen years ago?" And by 1860, with millions of Americans convinced that slavery was an evil, open insurrection by John Brown brought more public support than had the mere words of Garrison thirty years before.

This is not to say that extremists may not drive possible allies from their movement. But this is generally not because of the ferocity of their attack on an institution which is the object of general dislike, but because of their insertion of other issues which do not touch public sensibilities as much. Theodore Weld, an effective Midwestern abolitionist, who was marvelous at organizing abolitionist societies in Ohio, criticized Garrison for his violent attacks on the clergy, for his anarchist utterances against government in general, and for his insistence on bringing many other issues—women's rights, pacifism, etc.—into the antislavery fight. For marginal supporters, such side issues may bring alienation. Whether such estrangement would be significant enough to offset the general social value of having one important issue ride on the back of another, is another question.

Afterword

The changing image of Garrison in historical writing suggests the extent to which he has become a symbolic figure, who is reevaluated as attitudes change toward the principles he is thought to represent. He is, first of all, the personification of white racial egalitarianism, and hence, as we have seen, his stock fell and then rose in response to changing white attitudes toward the Negro. He represents also the kind of uncompromising radicalism that refuses to operate within the established political system, and therefore his image in any period is an indicator of prevailing views about how reformers or radicals should behave. Undoubtedly Garrison will continue to be evaluated by moral and ideological standards as long as the race problem remains a center of concern and men continue to disagree about how to achieve fundamental changes in their society.

There is another Garrison, however, who has not received enough attention from historians. This is the Garrison who was a man of his time, produced by special circumstances and functioning in a context that was unlike our own. Recapturing the historical Garrison is neither an easy task nor one that is likely to be welcomed by those who regard him as a symbol. The historian who argues that Garrison had motivations which we cannot share or ideas in which we no longer believe may well be attacked by neo-abolitionists as a covert enemy of the great *enduring* principles that Garrison represents. But to allow the discussion of Garrison to hinge entirely on moral and ideological judgments or to focus exclusively on his symbolic value for our time is to limit our ability to understand the man and his age. An effort to describe the social and psychological pressures that produced such a man need not derive from a desire to belittle him. Erik Erikson did not diminish Luther by describing him as a great man who went through a psychological crisis, the nature of which was determined by a combination of personal and historical factors.[1] Social and psychological explanation need not imply adverse judgment, if it is recognized from the outset that one is dealing, as one clearly would be in the case of Garrison, with no ordinary man, no mere reflection of social forces or

[1] Erik H. Erikson, *Young Man Luther* (New York, 1962).

typical neurotic patterns, and if we also acknowledge that a man may be right—even triumphantly right—for complex and unacknowledged reasons.

It seems likely then that new meanings for Garrison's career will come not from merely asserting that he was right or wrong, but from new and more sophisticated efforts to understand him. There is an opportunity here for the methodologically adventurous historian who is willing to raise the question of motivation, not from a desire to discredit a radical, but simply because he wishes to learn more about how a special kind of man responds, on the deepest personal level, to the crisis of his times.

Bibliographical Note

The best source for detailed information on Garrison and for extensive quotations from his writings and speeches is Wendell Phillips Garrison and Francis Jackson Garrison, *William Lloyd Garrison: The Story of His Life*, 4 vols. (New York, 1885–89). An excellent recent anthology of selections from *The Liberator* is Truman Nelson, ed., *Documents of Upheaval* (New York, 1966). *Selections from the Writings and Speeches of William Lloyd Garrison* (Boston, 1852) is an early collection of Garrison's utterances. Important biographies of Garrison, in addition to the one by his sons Wendell and Francis and those by Chapman, Nye, and Thomas (from which selections appear in this volume), are Oliver Johnson, *William Lloyd Garrison and his Times* (Boston, 1881), written by a long-time associate of Garrison's; Ralph Korngold, *Two Friends of Man* (Boston, 1950), a double biography of Garrison and of Wendell Phillips that began the current re-examination of the abolitionists; and Walter M. Merrill, *Against Wind and Tide* (Cambridge, Mass., 1963), a solid and creditable recent study. Garrison, of course, figures prominently in such general discussions of the abolitionist movement as A. B. Hart, *Slavery and Abolition* (New York, 1906), A. Y. Lloyd, *The Slavery Controversy, 1831–1860* (Chapel Hill, 1939), Louis B. Filler, *The Crusade Against Slavery* (New York, 1960), Dwight L. Dumond, *Antislavery* (Ann Arbor, 1961), and James M. McPherson, *The Struggle for Equality: Abolitionists and the Negro in the Civil War and Reconstruction* (Princeton, 1964).

Index